Empowered Citizens, Informed Consumers and Skilled Workers

DESIGNING EDUCATION AND SKILLS POLICIES FOR A SUSTAINABLE FUTURE

OECD

BETTER POLICIES FOR BETTER LIVES

Please cite this publication as:
OECD (2025), *Empowered Citizens, Informed Consumers and Skilled Workers: Designing Education and Skills Policies for a Sustainable Future*, OECD Publishing, Paris, https://doi.org/10.1787/311cdbeb-en.

ISBN 978-92-64-92516-8 (print)
ISBN 978-92-64-93232-6 (PDF)
ISBN 978-92-64-95728-2 (HTML)

Photo credits: Cover © Oleksii Sidorov/Shutterstock.com.

Corrigenda to OECD publications may be found at: https://www.oecd.org/en/publications/support/corrigenda.html.

Foreword

The challenges posed by climate change, biodiversity loss, and environmental degradation have become defining issues of our time. These crises are global in scope, affecting all regions of the planet, with impacts felt across all sectors of society. Facing these daunting challenges requires rethinking how we engage with the environment and, more deeply, how human systems in general operate.

At the heart of this transformative effort is education.

Education has the capacity to reshape our understanding of the world around us. It enables individuals to grasp the complexities of environmental systems, understand the interconnectedness of ecological, social, and economic factors, and ultimately take informed and responsible action. As this report outlines, education—both formal and informal—plays a crucial role in cultivating the awareness, knowledge, and skills needed to address the environmental challenges we face.

This report highlights how education and training policies can foster individual and collective agency, influence socio-behavioural change, and build skills that empower individuals, communities, and nations to engage in sustainable practices. It provides actionable insights and recommendations on how to incorporate sustainability into education and skills policies in a way that empowers learners at different life stages to contribute individually and collectively to a more sustainable future.

Across its various Directorates, the OECD is scaling up and mainstreaming its support to countries in navigating the climate challenge. This report is part of that effort. It brings together expertise from the Directorate for Education and Skills and the Environment Directorate with contributions from Directorates across the house. We hope that the insights presented here will inspire deeper reflection and action as we work together to create a future where people and planet can thrive in harmony.

The report was prepared as part of the OECD's Education Policies for a Sustainable Future project led by Deborah Nusche in the Directorate for Education and Skills. The analysis was conducted by a cross-directorate team at the OECD, bringing together expertise from the Directorate for Education and Skills and the Environment Directorate. The lead authors for the report are Deborah Nusche and François Staring from the Directorate for Education and Skills and Marcia Rocha and Cian Montague from the Environment Directorate. The report was prepared under the responsibility of Tia Loukkola, Head of the Innovation and Measuring Progress Division in the Directorate for Education and Skills and Andreas Schleicher, Director of Education and Skills.

This report contributes to the OECD Horizontal Project on Climate and Economic Resilience (Net Zero+).

Acknowledgements

The analysis was conducted by a cross-directorate team at the OECD, bringing together expertise from the Directorate for Education and Skills (EDU) and the Environment Directorate (ENV), as well as input from the Centre for Entrepreneurship, SMEs, Regions and Cities (CFE), the Centre for Skills (SKC), the Development Centre (DEV), the Development Co-operation Directorate (DCD), the Directorate for Employment, Labour and Social Affairs (ELS), the Directorate for Public Governance (GOV), the Directorate for Science, Technology and Innovation (STI), the Economics Department (ECO) and the International Energy Agency (IEA).

The authors are grateful to the many OECD colleagues who provided substantial contributions to the report. Data analysis in Chapter 1 was performed in collaboration with Gara Rojas Gonzáles, Jaione González Yubero and Yanjun Guo. Katherine Hassett and Olof Bystrom supported and reviewed data analysis on the OECD Survey on Environmental Policy and Individual Behaviour Change (EPIC); Noémie Le Donné and Gemma Coleman reviewed analysis of data from the OECD Survey of Social and Emotional Skills (SSES); and Daniel Salinas reviewed analysis of data from the OECD Programme of International Student Assessment (PISA). Manuela Fitzpatrick and Jason McGrath prepared Box 1.8 on the Leaving Certificate Climate Action and Sustainable Development in Ireland. The authors would also like to thank the following OECD and IEA colleagues for their review and insightful comments: Francesca Borgonovi, Magdalena Burtscher, Joanne Caddy, Malgorzata Kuczera, Jan Maarse, Marc Fuster Rabella, Rebecca Ruff, Pablo Shah, Michele Tuccio, Marieke Vandeweyer.

The comments and suggestions from external reviewers and contributors are also gratefully acknowledged, including from: Owen Gaffney (Chief Impact Officer, Nobel Prize Outreach and Co-lead, Earth4All), Ulrike Pisiotis (Policy Officer, European Commission), Matthew Pye (Head of Philosophy, European School Brussels II, Founder of The Climate Academy), Russel Tytler (Deakin Distinguished Professor and Chair of Science Education, FASSA, Deakin University).

The authors are grateful for the oversight, review, information and comments provided by the OECD's Education Policy Committee (EDPC). Special thanks are due to Radboud Dam, Marit van de Mortel and Rien Rouw from the Ministry of Education, Science and Culture, Netherlands; Patrizia Jankovic from the Ministry of Education, Austria; Geoffroy Libertiaux and Dominique Denis from the Fédération Wallonie-Bruxelles, Belgium; and Aoife Mitchell, Ian Mulholland, and Leona DeKhors from the Department of Education, Ireland, for providing country-specific information and reviewing policy examples from their countries. Financial support from the Ministry of Education, Science and Culture, Netherlands is gratefully acknowledged.

Within the OECD's Directorate for Education and Skills, the report was prepared for publication by Kebure Assefa and Jessica Bouton. Rachel Linden and Sasha Ramirez-Hughes offered editorial, publications and communications advice.

Editorial

Aligning Education and Skills for a Sustainable Future

In the face of unprecedented environmental challenges, the role of education has never been more critical. While awareness of climate change has grown across societies, the depth of understanding around its causes and potential solutions remains uneven. 71% of adults in G20 countries support immediate action on climate change. Yet, while the urgency is recognised, fewer individuals express a sense of personal responsibility for mitigating the climate crisis or engage in sustainable actions that could make a difference. Education systems hold the key to transforming this situation. By fostering deeper comprehension of interrelated social and environmental issues and their solutions, schools, universities, and vocational training programmes can help shape a generation more equipped to tackle climate challenges head-on.

The need for tailored educational strategies is clear when we examine the lifecycle perspective. As this report shows, environmental interest dips in adolescence, only to rise again in early adulthood. This decline during secondary education suggests that sustainability education is often too fragmented and repetitive to engage young people. Adolescents, who are ready for complex and systemic understandings of global issues, are not being adequately challenged by current sustainability curricula. To counter this, we must develop more integrated and engaging educational frameworks that align with their developmental needs, providing them with the tools to understand and act on the complexities of climate change.

For adults, recent graduates seem better informed about human contributions to climate change, possibly due to their exposure to more robust sustainability content during their schooling. However, socioeconomic factors, such as job sector and economic vulnerability, also play a significant role in shaping one's understanding of climate issues. In fact, while those from more advantaged backgrounds report higher levels of climate concern and engagement, their carbon footprints are often larger than those of less affluent groups. This paradox underscores the need for educational strategies that promote not just awareness, but meaningful behavioural change across all social strata.

Looking to the future, the green transition is set to reshape the global labour market. As countries strive towards net-zero emissions, some sectors will shrink while others will grow, creating demand for new skills and competencies. Already, high-skill green jobs are offering attractive employment options, but these are mostly concentrated in urban areas and require advanced qualifications. By contrast, low-skill green jobs, often in rural areas, tend to be insecure and poorly paid, making them less appealing to lower-educated workers. Without proactive policy intervention, the green transition risks exacerbating existing inequalities.

Vocational education and training (VET) and higher education must take centre stage in addressing these challenges. The current pace of upskilling and reskilling is woefully inadequate, with only 40% of adults across OECD countries participating in formal or non-formal learning for job-related purposes. Workers in high-emission industries and vulnerable sectors are training significantly less than others, heightening their risk of being left behind in the green economy. Policymakers must ensure that reskilling and upskilling opportunities are both accessible and relevant, with a focus on those most vulnerable to economic displacement.

It is encouraging to see that many countries are beginning to prioritise sustainability within their education and training agendas. However, the reality is that only half of OECD education ministries currently identify greener and fairer societies as a policy focus for post-secondary education. More attention needs to be paid to vocational and tertiary levels, particularly in aligning curricula with the demands of a rapidly greening economy.

The path forward is clear. Education systems must be designed not only to impart knowledge but also to equip learners with the skills necessary to adapt to and drive the green transition. This requires collaboration between educational institutions, governments, and industries to ensure that skills provision is strategically aligned with both regional needs and national priorities. Upskilling and reskilling must be made a policy priority, ensuring that the most vulnerable workers are not left behind in the rush towards sustainability.

As the climate crisis continues to unfold, it is essential that education and training systems evolve to meet the moment. The solutions are within reach, but they require an integrated, lifecycle approach to sustainability education, combined with policies that promote equitable access to skills development. In doing so, we can create a future where all individuals, regardless of their background or location, are empowered to contribute to a sustainable and resilient global economy.

Andreas Schleicher
Director for the Directorate for Education and Skills and Special Advisor on Education Policy to the Secretary General

Table of contents

Tables

Figures

Boxes

Executive summary

Unchecked, the interrelated planetary crises of climate change, biodiversity loss and pollution have the potential to impact every dimension of human existence, imperiling lives, livelihoods, and the social and economic stability of countries and regions, alongside the natural environment on which we all depend. This report highlights that education and training systems are deeply intertwined with these challenges, both as vulnerable to the impacts of these socio-ecological crises, and as crucial in shaping behaviours, collective action and skills that can support sustainable societies and greening economies.

Key findings

The report argues for a holistic, lifecycle approach to sustainability education that spans from compulsory schooling through to vocational education and training, higher education and lifelong learning. While compulsory education can potentially reach all children and youth at a critical developmental age and lay the foundation for widespread change, focussing on adult education is equally important. Given the urgency of the climate crisis and the speed of change in societies and economies, supporting relevant lifelong learning across education levels, sectors and settings is the only way to ensuring effective societal responses within the timeframes required.

Citizens' agency, i.e. the ability of individuals to positively shape their own lives and the world around them, is at the heart of the report. In the context of sustainability challenges, agency must be grounded in a solid understanding of the relationships between ecological and social systems and a range of transversal competencies, including scientific and systems thinking and capacity for collective action. Fostering these competencies across the lifecycle requires embedding them across curricula, qualifications and study programmes, bringing place-based, interdisciplinary and experiential approaches to scale, and building bridges across formal, non-formal and informal learning opportunities.

The focus on individual and collective agency should not be understood as passing the responsibility for climate mitigation from governments to individuals and communities. Instead, it reflects that socio-behavioural change, alongside stringent policies and accountability, is an essential part of all pathways to net-zero carbon emissions, and one over which education and training systems have considerable leverage. While socio-behavioural change matters, it must be embedded in a systemic perspective. Education and skills approaches should offer learners age-appropriate tools to situate their own action with understanding of broader sectoral and system changes.

Beyond essential sustainability competencies, education and skills strategies must focus on fostering the technical and transversal skills that allow individuals to pursue sustainable careers and benefit from the green transition. The policies countries are adopting globally to achieve net-zero greenhouse gas emissions are reshaping local labour markets by reducing jobs in high-emission industries, creating new opportunities in climate-friendly sectors, and transforming many existing occupations. Skills and labour shortages are projected for key green sectors, which risks slowing down progress towards climate goals and may exacerbate inequalities if there is insufficient attention to helping workers transition out of emission-intensive sectors.

Education and skills policies are crucial to ensuring a just transition. The green transition is generating high-quality jobs, but these are primarily concentrated in high-skill occupations. By contrast, low-skill green-driven jobs tend to offer lower wages and less job security than other low-skill occupations, making them less appealing for lower-educated workers. This highlights the critical role of education and skills policies in supporting the transition, alongside labour market policies to enhance the quality of these jobs.

Skills development policies to date are not keeping up with the required pace of change. On average across OECD countries, only around four in ten adults participate in formal or non-formal learning for job-related reasons, and workers in high-emissions occupations tend to train significantly less than other workers. Given their close connection to the labour market, vocational education and training (VET), higher and adult education systems are uniquely positioned to provide relevant initial programmes and reskilling and upskilling opportunities for the green transition. Stronger alignment between these different sectors and collaboration of key stakeholders around a common vision for skills development will be key to meeting the challenges of the green transition.

Key recommendations

1. **Adapt curricula, qualifications and study programmes.** To support curriculum adaptation, governments can foster collaboration across key stakeholders to map the extent to which sustainability competencies, and key technical and transversal skills, are covered in curricula and qualifications, identify gap areas and develop guidance to support curriculum adaptation.
2. **Upskill educators across levels and sectors of education:** Mainstreaming sustainability in initial teacher education, and in continuing professional learning opportunities for educators across schools, vocational and higher education, can help break down silos and disseminate innovative and interdisciplinary teaching approaches that align with sustainability goals and the needs of green industries.
3. **Bring place-based approaches to scale.** Place-based and collaborative practices, including whole-institution approaches and local partnerships, can support inclusion and foster agency for socio-behavioural change via experiential learning. Governments can help bring effective practice to scale by providing frameworks, resources, and incentives, such as green labelling programmes.
4. **Build bridges across formal, non-formal and informal learning.** Formal education providers, in particular higher education institutions, can play a key role in science communication, consumer education and awareness-raising campaigns around climate change. Governments can enhance these links, for example by investing in support centres for science communication.
5. **Strengthen skills assessment and anticipation**. Considering the impact of net-zero targets and environmental policies on labour market and skills demands is key to inform national skills strategies. Governments can support effective skills assessment and anticipation processes by ensuring broad stakeholder involvement and tailoring approaches to regional contexts.
6. **Enhance "green" career guidance.** Sustainability-oriented career guidance can empower individuals to transform their motivation to act into sustainable careers, connect educational pathways with broader social and environmental goals, and support workers in transitioning out of declining industries and towards high-quality jobs in green sectors.
7. **Develop a coherent and inclusive skills delivery landscape across vocational, higher and adult education.** Governments can facilitate co-operation and strategic alignment across post-secondary education providers and industries, regional authorities and other relevant actors to adapt initial programme offers, expand upskilling and reskilling opportunities and remove barriers to participation in training.

1 Overview

In 2023, global average temperatures had reached 1.45°C (with a margin of uncertainty of ±0.12°C) above pre-industrial levels (WMO, 2024[1]). A series of climate impacts accompanied this record high temperature increase. Marine heatwaves affected nearly one-third of the global ocean, harming ecosystems and food systems. The world's most important glaciers experienced unprecedented ice loss, driven by extreme melt in North America and Europe. Extreme weather events—floods, cyclones, heatwaves, and wildfires—had far-reaching socio-economic impacts, exacerbating acute food insecurity. Meanwhile, global mean sea level surged to a record high due to ocean warming and glacier/ice sheet melting (WMO, 2024[1]). In addition, there is today unequivocal evidence that the planet is approaching so-called 'Earth tipping points', where beyond certain thresholds, sub-systems of the planet undergo a system change, often in an abrupt and irreversible manner, with negative impacts that can cascade through socio-economic systems. Some of these tipping points, such as the West Antarctic and the Greenland ice sheets, are at risk of being crossed at much lower levels of warming—and therefore much sooner—than previously thought (Armstrong McKay et al., 2022[2]; OECD, 2022[3]).

The Paris Agreement, a legally binding international treaty on climate change adopted by 196 Parties at the 21st Conference of Parties (COP 21) in Paris, seeks to hold the increase of global average temperature to well-below 2°C, while pursuing efforts to limit it to 1.5°CT[1] (Paris Agreement, 2015[4]). Addressing the climate change challenge requires responses at various levels across different sectors of the economy to mitigate increasing threats to humanity and the environment, and to adapt to both current and future impacts. Indeed, meeting the goals of the Agreement calls for a profound transformation in the way societies and economies function. This shift goes beyond incremental changes and instead requires systemic changes in critical sectors such as transport, energy, food and agricultural systems to ensure sustainability and resilience. (IPCC, 2022[5]). Progress in tackling the climate crisis has been made globally since the Paris Agreement was adopted, albeit at a largely slower pace and scale than necessary to meet the Agreement's goals. To promote the change at the necessary scale and pace, it is crucial to reflect both on what gaps and obstacles exist in current systems, as well as on how the world can build on observed advancements to date.

The education and training sector is intrinsically linked with climate and other environmental challenges in several ways. First, the education and training systems are vulnerable to the impacts of these crises. Around half of the 7 5 million children who have their education disrupted each year do so as a result of climate-related extreme events and natural disasters, including heat waves, floods, as well as disease outbreaks (Theirworld, 2018[6]; World Economic Forum, 2023[7]; UNESCO, 2024[8]). The direct consequences of these include the destruction of infrastructure, including education institutions, and the loss of life or injuries, including among students, parents, and school staff. While low-income countries are more impacted by extreme weather events, direct climate risks are also increasing in high-income countries. In addition, climate change affects education through internal and cross-border displacement, as well as impacts on livelihoods and health. Evidence indicates that, extreme temperatures, for example, affect learning and cognitive potential (Horvath and Borgonovi, 2022[9]; Nusche, Fuster Rabella and Lauterbach, 2024[10]). All these effects are exacerbated by socio-economic factors and impacts are disproportionately felt amongst vulnerable communities and populations (IPCC, 2022[11]).

Second, education and training are instrumental in shaping behaviours that underpin climate action and sustainability. Education and skills policies have the potential to serve as a catalyst for fostering environmental awareness and critical thinking, equipping individuals with the knowledge and skills necessary to comprehend interconnectedness of global systems and the complexities of climate and environmental challenges. By bridging the gap between knowledge of the climate and other environmental challenges and the potential solutions for these challenges, education and training provide valuable insights, and help enable individuals to adopt sustainable behaviours and actively participate in shaping policies and practices that support sustainability. Through promoting agency and civic engagement, education can also encourage proactive involvement in addressing environmental issues, ultimately driving the cultural shifts and social, political and economic changes essential for tackling climate change and other environmental challenges.

Finally, education and training play a crucial role in skills development, particularly as labour markets transition in response to climate and other environmental challenges. The transition to an inclusive green economy can serve as a robust engine for growth and a significant driver of decent work creation across developing, emerging, and advanced economies (van der Ree, 2019[12]). Ensuring a sustainable planet requires policies that secure long-term employment and social well-being, presenting both challenges and opportunities for policymakers as they strive to reshape job markets towards greener economies. This dynamic landscape demands a workforce equipped with the necessary skills, underscoring the importance of education and skills policies in preparing individuals for the evolving demands of sustainable markets and jobs. There is a need therefore to enhance the strategic importance of the sector for the transition to greener societies and a safer future (OECD, 2023[13]; OECD, 2023[14]).

This report seeks to provide further understanding on the role education and training systems can play in fostering transformative change and building resilient societies by (1) empowering citizens and communities for action, (2) fostering informed consumption and lifestyle choices and (3) equipping individuals with the skills needed for changing labour markets in response to the greening of economies and societies. Chapter 2 consolidates evidence on the ways in which education policies can promote socio-behavioural change to foster environmental sustainability and resilience in society at large, while Chapter 3 focusses on the role of education and training policies in supporting the green transition of economies, from a perspective of skills development. Each Chapter concludes with a set of policy options that, taken together, aim to support countries in designing coherent, flexible and inclusive education and skills systems, where individuals of all ages and backgrounds are supported in shaping a sustainable future and making the most of the opportunities offered by the green transition.

References

Armstrong McKay, D. et al. (2022), "Exceeding 1.5°C global warming could trigger multiple climate tipping points", *Science*, Vol. 377/6611, https://doi.org/10.1126/science.abn7950. [2]

Horvath, D. and F. Borgonovi (2022), "Global warming, pollution and cognitive developments: The effects of high pollution and temperature levels on cognitive ability throughout the life course", *OECD Social, Employment and Migration Working Papers*, No. 269, OECD Publishing, Paris, https://doi.org/10.1787/319b9a1f-en. [9]

IPCC (2022), "Summary for Policymakers", in P.R. Shukla et al. (eds.), *Climate Change 2022: Mitigation of Climate Change. Contribution of Working Group III to the Sixth Assessment Report of the Intergovernmental Panel on Climate Change*, Cambridge University Press, Cambridge, United Kingdom and New York, NY, USA. [5]

IPCC (2022), "Summary for Policymakers", in H.-O. Pörtner et al. (eds.), *Climate Change 2022: Impacts, Adaptation, and Vulnerability. Contribution of Working Group II to the Sixth Assessment Report of the Intergovernmental Panel on Climate Change . In Press.*, Cambridge University Press. [11]

Nusche, D., M. Fuster Rabella and S. Lauterbach (2024), "Rethinking education in the context of climate change: Leverage points for transformative change", *OECD Education Working Papers*, No. 307, OECD Publishing, Paris, https://doi.org/10.1787/f14c8a81-en. [10]

OECD (2023), *Education Policy Outlook 2023: Empowering All Learners to Go Green*, OECD Publishing, Paris, https://doi.org/10.1787/f5063653-en. [14]

OECD (2023), *OECD Skills Outlook 2023: Skills for a Resilient Green and Digital Transition*, OECD Publishing, Paris, https://doi.org/10.1787/27452f29-en. [13]

OECD (2022), *Climate Tipping Points: Insights for Effective Policy Action*, OECD Publishing, Paris, https://doi.org/10.1787/abc5a69e-en. [3]

Paris Agreement (2015), *15 December 2015*, United Nations Treaty Collection Certified True Copies (CTCs) of Multilateral Treaties Deposited with the Secretary-General Chapter XXVII.7.d, https://treaties.un.org/pages/ViewDetails.aspx?src=TREATY&mtdsg_no=XXVII-7-d&chapter=27 (accessed on 28 April 2020). [4]

Theirworld (2018), *Safe Schools: The Hidden Crisis*, http://s3.amazonaws.com/theirworld-site-resources/Reports/Theirworld-Report-Safe-Schools-December-2018.pdf (accessed on 19 June 2024). [6]

UNESCO (2024), *Education and climate change: learning to act for people and planet*, https://unesdoc.unesco.org/ark:/48223/pf0000389801 (accessed on 14 June 2024). [8]

van der Ree, K. (2019), "Encourager les emplois verts : le travail décent dans la transition vers des économies vertes et à faible émission de carbone, Promoting Green Jobs: Decent Work in the Transition to Low-Carbon, Green Economies, Fomento de los empleos verdes: trabajo decente en la transición hacia economías verdes y bajas en carbono", *Revue internationale de politique de développement* 11, pp. 248-271, https://doi.org/10.4000/poldev.3107. [12]

WMO (2024), *State of the Global Climate 2023*, World Metereological Organization, Geneva. [1]

World Economic Forum (2023), *The climate crisis disrupts 40 million children's education every year. Here's how we could fix it*, https://www.weforum.org/agenda/2023/02/girls-education-climate-crisis-educational-disruption-resilience/ (accessed on 19 June 2024). [7]

Notes

1 While the nearing or even potential breach of 1.5°C threshold in the near future does not imply a permanent exceedance of the 1.5°C limit set by the Paris Agreement—which refers to long-term warming over decades—it is a matter of serious concern which alerts to the need of bold, stringent and immediate action on climate.

2 Fostering behavioural and social change for a sustainable future: a lifelong learning approach

The role of socio-behavioural change in addressing the climate crisis

Achieving a sustainable future for all requires rapid and far-reaching transformations across all sectors and systems (IPCC, 2022[1]). Sector transformation refers to significant changes within a specific area of the economy or society, whereas system transformation refers to broad and integrated changes across multiple interconnected sectors and their interactions within broader social, economic, and ecological contexts.

Some sectors such as energy, industry and agriculture are critical because they are among the most significant contributors to greenhouse gas (GHG) emissions and thus to climate change. Figure 2.1 shows emissions trends by sectors of the economy between 1990 and 2019 and shows that globally, GHG emissions continued to rise across all sectors and subsectors, with the most rapid increases observed in transport and industry. In 2019, the energy sector accounted for 34% of global GHG emissions, industry contributed 24%, agriculture, forestry, and other land use (AFOLU) were responsible for 22%, transport produced 15% and buildings accounted for 5.6%.

Figure 2.1. Trends in global emissions by sector of the economy

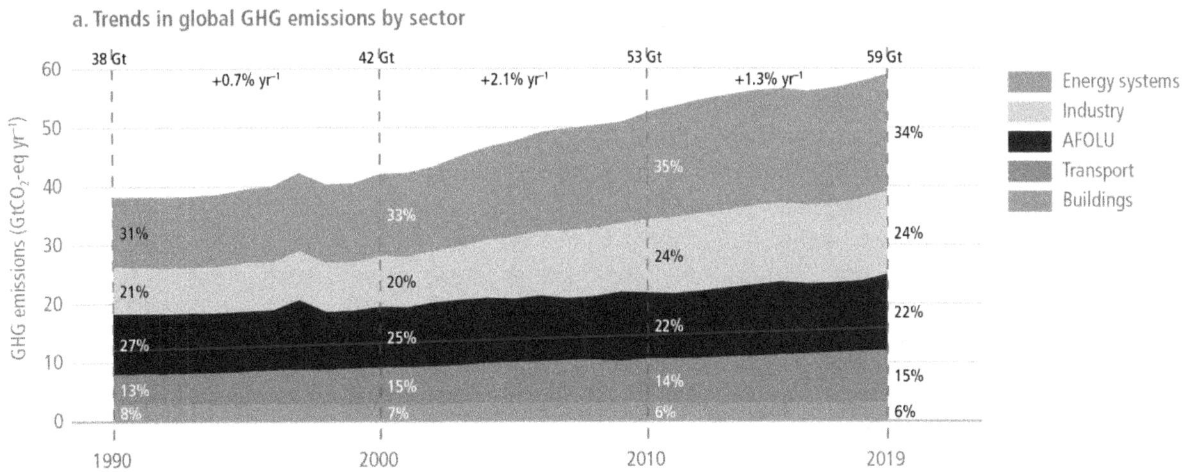

Source: (Dhakal et al., 2022[2]) "Emissions Trends and Drivers", in IPCC, 2022: Climate Change 2022 - Mitigation of Climate Change, Cambridge University Press, https://doi.org/10.1017/9781009157926.004.

Sector transformation or transition typically focuses on improving the efficiency and sustainability of practices within a particular sector, through for example adopting new technologies, policies, and practices that reduce GHG emissions and enhance resilience to climate impacts within that sector. Human-induced climate change results, however, from over a century of net GHG emissions stemming from unsustainable patterns of consumption and production (IPCC, 2023[3]), which are not restricted or exclusive to a particular sector.

Beyond changes in particular sectors, economic and social systems in general thus need to transform. System transformation approaches recognise that sectors do not operate in isolation and aim to reconfigure entire networks and relationships to create a more sustainable, resilient, and equitable society. This entails taking a systems-thinking approach where synergies and trade-offs across sectors are considered through a transdisciplinary approach, leveraging the linkages between mitigation, adaptation, and sustainable development (von Stechow et al., 2015[4]; Rogelj et al., 2018[5]). Systems thinking supports a dynamic analytical approach to environmental crises by considering the interconnectedness, feedback loops, and dynamic complexity of climate change.

In energy systems, this means, for example, dramatically reducing fossil fuel use, diversifying energy generation with renewables, adopting carbon capture technologies and extensive electrification (IPCC, 2023[3]). In the industry sector, reducing GHG emissions requires improving energy and materials efficiency and establishing circular material flows (Ibid). For the AFOLU sector, adopting sustainable farming practices, improving livestock management, conservation and restoration of forests are critical for reducing sectoral emissions (Ibid). These measures need to be combined with measures that shift development pathways as a whole. This includes broader sectoral policies to induce emissions reductions by all actors along the supply chain such as producers, transporters and retailers, as well as policies that induce lifestyle or consumption changes in end users (Ibid).

Demand-side mitigation strategies that change households' behavioural choices can reduce global GHG emissions in end-use sectors by 40–80% by 2050 (Creutzig et al., 2021[6]). Even if quantitative estimates of mitigation potential associated with behavioural change vary in the literature, studies broadly converge on the most effective behavioural changes, which can be found primarily in the food, mobility and housing sectors. Ivanova et al. (2020[7]) compare the mitigation potential of various consumption options and find that living car-free, switching to electric vehicles, reducing air travel, adopting a vegan diet, and using renewable electricity, are among the behavioural changes with the highest mitigation potential. For instance, a global transition to plant-based diets has the potential to reduce diet-related land use by 76% and diet-related GHG emissions by 49% (Gibbs and Cappuccio, 2022[8]).

While behavioural changes are essential in addressing climate change, they cannot replace stringent policies at national, sub-national, and local levels. Policies are crucial because they establish the structural and systemic changes necessary to address the root causes of climate change, e.g. by ending fossil fuel support and providing low-carbon infrastructure, thereby ensuring long-term, scalable impact beyond individual actions. In addition, a dynamic relationship exists between behaviour and policy, where policies shape and regulate behaviour by setting standards and creating incentives or disincentives for sustainable practices, while widespread behavioural changes and advocacy can drive policy development by generating public demand for stronger environmental regulations and accountability. Even when individuals face practical barriers to adopt sustainable behaviours, informed intention to act can still play a crucial role in shaping public discourse and encouraging policymakers to adapt and respond.

Indeed, civic engagement plays a crucial role in fostering societal consensus and lowering obstacles to broader policy action on adaptation, mitigation, and sustainable development. (Pörtner et al., 2022[9]). Social and civic actions, such as activism, legal action, and policy advocacy, are highly effective in contributing to systems change. While quantifying the impact of social and civic actions on systems change is challenging, studies have shown a robust positive effect of such action through a range of qualitative indicators (Khatibi et al., 2021[10]; Sato M et al., 2023[11]). For example, it has been shown that legal action and climate litigation risk is considered to be a significant financial risk by lenders, regulators, and governments (Sato M et al., 2023[11]).

Education is fundamental in empowering individuals to make informed decisions and act on climate change, be it in their consumption and lifestyle choices or in their civic and political engagement. Indeed, the universal reach of education systems makes formal education a key factor in influencing behaviours, norms and values systems (OECD, 2023[12]; Nusche, Fuster Rabella and Lauterbach, 2024[13]). Elements that are covered in compulsory education can potentially reach all youth at a critical developmental age and lay the foundation for widespread change (Pereira and Freire, 2021[14]; Wynes and Nicholas, 2017[15]). Although young people enrolled in school education have a lower environmental footprint and less decision-making power than adults, education is key to shaping subsequent consumption behaviour and civic engagement, as well as career choices (the latter will be addressed in Chapter 2).

While some effects of education unfold only in the medium- and long-term, other impacts of education can materialise much faster. For example, over the last decade, youth-led initiatives have become increasingly visible around the world (Pereira and Freire, 2021[14]; Han and Ahn, 2020[16]). The surge in climate movements and youth civic engagement on environmental and sustainability issues are identified as one of the five major positive shifts observed in the last decade that contribute to a more climate-safe trajectory (Roeser et al., 2023[17]). Indeed, research indicates that normative change, i.e. change in what is perceived as normal or morally acceptable, can catalyse significant transformations in legislation, policy, and behaviour. Normative change often begins with a normative challenge, where practices once deemed normal are increasingly viewed as morally unacceptable. Analysis shows that social movements, such as youth-led climate initiatives, have created normative challenges that support the need for shifts across societies (Spaiser, Nisbett and Stefan, 2022[18]).

In addition, the multiplying effects of school education are likely to touch families, communities and social networks via peer effects, intergenerational exchange and local collaboration. For example, results from the OECD's Programme for International Student Assessment (PISA) indicate that young people's pro-environmental engagement is interrelated with the level of engagement of their parents and peers (OECD, 2022[19]; OECD, 2023[12]). While the influence of parental values on their children is not surprising, there are indications that this influence can run both ways, with shifts in students' knowledge, attitudes and behaviours also influencing those of their parents (Damerell, Howe and Milner-Gulland, 2013[20]; Lawson et al., 2019[21]).

However, focusing on compulsory schooling is not enough. To avoid the most catastrophic impacts of climate change, wide-reaching societal and economic changes are critical this decade and require developing relevant educational offers and opportunities for adults. Adult education takes place in formal vocational education and training (VET) and higher education settings as well as through various non-formal and informal settings. Spreading educational offers and opportunities across different education levels, sectors and settings seems the most effective way to ensuring cross-generational awareness and action.

At the same time, the time pressures for action should not be interpreted as a reason to diminish attention to younger generations. Educating children remains critical as future generations will inherit a world increasingly shaped by climate change. Indeed, a climate change-free world is no longer possible, and they must be prepared not only to continue to reduce emissions but also to navigate its inevitable impacts, which will vary based on the actions taken today. For example, limiting warming to 1.5°C by the end of the century instead of 2°C can significantly reduce the frequency and intensity of extreme weather events, improve public health outcomes and give communities and ecosystems more time to adapt. Achieving this goal requires stringent action throughout the century to peak and decline global temperatures (IPCC, 2018[22]). For education, this means that every age group counts and that a holistic lifecycle approach to environmental, sustainability and climate change education is the only way forward.

The remainder of this chapter explores the role that education systems can play in fostering agency for socio-behavioural change at different ages and stages of learning. The focus on behavioural change and civic action should not be understood as passing the responsibility for climate mitigation from governments to individuals and communities. Instead, it is based on the understanding that socio-behavioural change is an essential part of all pathways to net-zero carbon emissions, and one over which education system have considerable leverage.

The intricate interactions between socio-behavioural change, policies and economic activity are highlighted throughout the chapter. This resonates with the 2022 OECD Declaration on Building Trust and Reinforcing Democracy, which highlights key role of public governance to take strong and urgent transformative action on climate and sustainable development and the need to build consensus and trust, including through meaningful participatory processes, for delivering internationally-agreed global goals (OECD, 2022[23])

Developing agency for socio-behavioural change: what does it take and where are we now?

Agency is the capacity to set goals, reflect, and take responsible actions to effect change. This concept is rooted in the belief that learners have both the ability and the will to positively influence their own lives and the world around them. Essentially, fostering agency involves empowering individuals to make meaningful decisions and take actions that drive their learning and impact their communities positively. It is about acting rather than being acted upon; shaping rather than being shaped; and making responsible decisions and choices rather than accepting those determined by others (OECD, 2019[24]; OECD, 2022[19]; OECD, 2021[25]).

Recent OECD (2024[26])survey data highlights declining levels of trust among citizens in their governments' capacity to tackle complex policy issues, such as climate change. In addition, only around 40% of people believe that the government balances the interests of different generations. Yet, OECD (2024[26])also finds that citizens who believe they have a say in government report higher levels of trust in national government (69%) than those who do not feel they have a say (22%). This large gap in trust levels highlights the need to foster citizens' sense of agency and participation.

Agency is a multi-facetted concept. In psychology, it is typically described in terms of having a high degree of self-efficacy, *i.e.* a high internal locus of control and a strong belief that one has the power to alter events. In a sociological perspective, agency is also explored in terms of how it is negotiated between individuals and groups (OECD, 2024[27]). While all individuals inherently have agency, not everyone has the same opportunities to exercise this agency. Indeed, agency is reflective not only of individuals' intentionality, values, preferences and capacity, but also of the constraints of the social and material environment that surrounds them (OECD, 2024[27]). In addition, the sense of agency that individuals experience is likely to be influenced by intersectional factors such as socio-economic background, age, gender and - for children in particular - prevalent parenting style, including the types of toys and games they are exposed to and the level of emancipative values in their families and communities (e.g. whether they are allowed to question dominant narratives) (OECD, 2024[27]).

Education can play a key role in empowering learners to use their agency, equipping them with the foundational knowledge, skills and attitudes that allow them to understand the world around them and see themselves as actors within it (OECD, 2021[25]; OECD, 2019[28]; OECD, 2022[19]). In the specific context of environmental and sustainability challenges, White et al. (2023[29]) describe the essential competencies that underlie what they call "agency in the Anthropocene[1], *i.e.* agency in an era where human activity is significantly altering Earth systems. These include:

- Understanding the impact of human interactions within Earth's systems;

- Making informed decisions to act, based on evaluation of diverse sources of evidence and application of creative and systems thinking to regenerate and sustain the environment; and
- Demonstrating respect for diverse perspectives, and hope, in seeking solutions to socio-ecological crises.

This definition of agency in the context of socio-environmental crises emphasises not just the ability to act, but the ability to do so based on a solid understanding of Earth systems and their interactions with human activity. This highlights the fact that individuals can only make informed decisions to act if they are sufficiently aware of, know about and understand environmental and sustainability challenges, including their causes and potential solutions. Going further, the definition highlights a range of key competencies that are essential in seeking solutions to socio-ecological crises, which resonate with various definitions of "sustainability competencies" developed across the world (see Box 2.4 later in this chapter).

Building on this broad definition of agency in the context of sustainability challenges, the remainder of this chapter reviews selected international indicators illustrating levels of understanding of socio-ecological challenges among different age groups, and analyses how these interact with learners' attitudes, consumption behaviour and civic engagement for sustainability.

Awareness, attitudes and action regarding climate change across the lifecycle

This section provides a snapshot of selected international indicators on awareness, attitudes and actions regarding environmental sustainability and climate change among different age groups in OECD and partner countries. Studies and data show that there may exist connections and mismatches between environmental knowledge/awareness, attitudes, and actions. Analysing these three elements, at different stages of individuals' lives, can offer a comprehensive understanding of the various opportunities and challenges that education and training systems must navigate to effectively support agency across the lifecycle.

Box 2.1. Methodology and data sources

The section draws on a variety of data sources including the OECD's Programme for International Student Assessment (PISA) Global Competence Assessment (2018) (OECD, 2022[19]), the European Social Survey (ESS) Round 8 (2016) (ESS, 2016[30]), the International Social Survey Programme (2020) (ISSP, 2020[31]), the OECD's Survey on Environmental Policies and Individual Behaviour Change (EPIC) (OECD, 2023[32]), and the *Earth for all survey 2024*, a comprehensive survey conducted in G20 countries examining attitudes to societal transformations, political and economic systems and planetary stewardship (Earth4All, 2024[33]). Part of the analysis in this section was developed in collaboration with the OECD's INES Network on Labour Market, Economic and Social Outcomes of Learning, more detailed information on underlying data sources and methodologies available in (OECD, 2024[34]).

Data is presented for various age groups and countries based on availability in the original data sources and associated reports. The data does not allow to compare results on awareness, attitudes and actions across different surveys, as the specific indicators and questions asked are similar but not the same. Survey implementation dates also vary, which is likely to have impacted on the exposure that respondents have had to public information, news reporting and activism regarding climate change. In particular, the ESS data (2016) and the OECD's PISA (2018) data predate significant factors influencing climate change awareness, such as certain prominent youth-led climate protests and the surge in media coverage of climate catastrophes (see Figure 2.11). In the absence of more recent data of comparable coverage and quality, they still offer relevant insights.

Awareness and depth of understanding

Awareness of socio-ecological issues pertains to an individual's understanding and perception of environmental conditions and sustainability, including anticipation of future developments. There are indications that young people generally consider themselves familiar with the challenges of climate change when they are approaching the end of compulsory education. In the OECD's Programme for International Student Assessment (PISA) 2018, almost 80% of students aged 15 years old reported knowing about or being very familiar with climate change and global warming on average across OECD countries (OECD, 2022[19]). At the same time, the data also show significant socio-economic variation. As shown in Figure 2.2, on average across OECD countries, the share of students displaying awareness of climate change and global warming among socio-economically advantaged students was 20 percentage points higher (at 88%) than among disadvantaged students (at 68%) (OECD, 2022[19])[2].

Figure 2.2. Environmental awareness, by student's socio-economic status

Percentage of 15-year-old students who reported knowing about or being very familiar with climate change and global warming

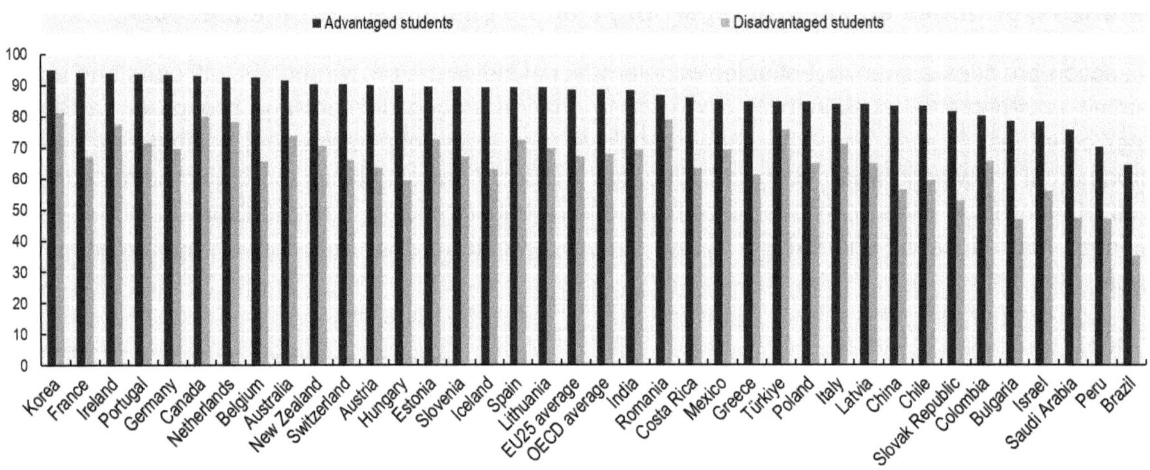

Source: (OECD, 2024[34]) Education at a Glance 2024: OECD Indicators, OECD Publishing, Paris, https://doi.org/10.1787/c00cad36-en, based on PISA 2018 data.

Widespread climate change awareness is not surprising given the surge in news coverage on the climate crisis over the last decade (see Figure 2.11 further below). But, in fact, awareness levels tell us little about the depth of knowledge and the understanding individuals have of the intricate relationships between ecological and human factors. Being aware of climate change does not necessarily mean having a solid scientific understanding of its magnitude, causes and potential solutions.

When asked to rate their actual knowledge and competence in explaining climate change and environmental issues, a smaller share of students reported feeling confident about their ability to articulate complex issues related to climate change: on average across the OECD, 63% of 15-year-old students reported that they could explain the impact of carbon-dioxide emissions on the environment easily or with some effort (OECD, 2022[19]).

Beyond self-reported levels of knowledge, the PISA 2018 survey also offers insights into students' actual proficiency in responding to environmental sustainability test items. The 2018 Global Competence assessment included 5 test units that assessed students' knowledge and skills related to both "natural resources and environmental risks" and "policies, practices and behaviours for environmental sustainability", i.e. both the ecological and social aspects of environmental challenges. The assessment was conducted in 26 countries and economies (of which 12 OECD countries). Results show that on average across countries and test units, less than 50% of students were able to answer sustainability items correctly, although there were variations across countries and across test units, as shown in Figure 2.3.

This shows that, among students nearing the end of compulsory education, knowledge about global sustainability issues as assessed in PISA 2018 is still highly variable. In terms of socio-economic status, performance in environmental sustainability was better among socio-economically advantaged than disadvantaged students in each of the 20 environmental sustainability items on average across countries and economies.

In the context of students' agency, it is of interest to know whether students are acquiring knowledge about potential solutions and competencies to reflect about solutions to complex climate challenges. Among the sustainability questions, the test unit on "rising sea levels" allows analysing students' understanding regarding potential solutions to a consequence of climate change. The question aimed to identify whether students were able to distinguish between (1) solutions that are long-term and address the root causes of climate change and (2) solutions that are short-term and adapt human environments to climate change. The analysis of responses shows that, on average across countries, 70% of students were able to correctly identify reducing GHG emissions as a long-term response and 60% of students were able to correctly identify building sea defences as a short-term response, indicating that many misunderstood building sea defences as a long-term response to the climate crisis[3].

Figure 2.3. Correct answers by students on environmental sustainability items

Average percentage 15-year-old students who correctly answered environmental sustainability items, across test units

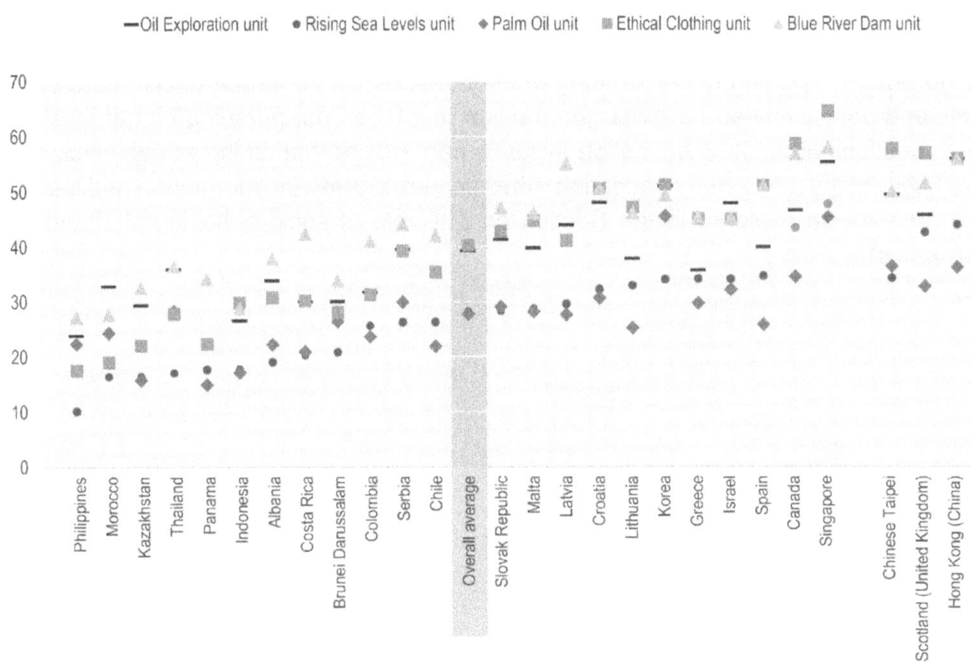

Note: Countries and economies are ranked in ascending order of the percentage of students who correctly responded the items under the Rising Sea levels unit.

Source: (OECD, 2022[19]) Are Students Ready to Take on Environmental Challenges?, PISA, OECD Publishing, Paris, https://doi.org/10.1787/8abe655c-en.

For adults, results from the European Social Survey (ESS) Round 8 (2016) (ESS, 2016[30]) and the International Social Survey Programme (ISSP) 2020 (ISSP, 2020[31]) offer some insights on the extent to which individuals beyond the age of compulsory education understand the causes of climate change. The European Social Survey included a question asking participants to identify the main causes of climate change. In response to this question, on average among the OECD countries participating in the survey, only 46% of 25-64-year-olds correctly identified human activity as the main cause of climate change.

At the same time, it is noteworthy that the share of individuals understanding human-induced climate change is higher on average among younger adults, with 53% of 18-24-year-olds selecting human activity as the main cause (OECD, 2024[34]). The shares are higher for the younger age group in nearly all OECD countries except Czechia, Hungary and Israel. The difference between age groups is most pronounced in Norway where 57% of 18-24-year-olds acknowledge that climate change is caused mainly or entirely by human activity, compared to only 37% of 25-64-year-olds (Table A6.2 in (OECD, 2024[34])). One explanation for the better understanding among younger individuals of the anthropogenic nature of climate change might be that recent graduates may have benefitted from more in-depth coverage of environmental and sustainability content as part of their formal education than older generations, but it is likely that other factors are also at play here, such as a stronger perceived exposure to climate risks and fewer vested interests in maintaining the status quo (Asai, Borgonovi and Wildi, 2022[35]).

The ESS data also allows to compare these responses by educational attainment levels for the 25-64 age group. A clear pattern emerges, where higher levels of education correlate with increased awareness of human-induced climate change in almost all countries (Figure 2.4). An average of only 38% of individuals with below upper secondary education indicated understanding that climate change is mainly or entirely caused by human activity, compared to 45% with upper secondary or post-secondary non-tertiary education, and 54% with tertiary education. For three non-European OECD countries - Korea, New Zealand and the United States - similar information is available from the International Social Survey Programme 2020. The emerging pattern from this data is less clear, but still evident in two of the three countries (Figure 2.4).

These low shares of individuals reporting understanding of the human-induced nature of climate change are concerning overall, and particularly so for older generations and those not pursuing higher levels of education. This raises questions about how education systems can ensure that all individuals, including those not pursuing post-secondary and tertiary education, have access to relevant information and lifelong learning opportunities (this will be explored in the Section on The role of socio-behavioural change in addressing the climate crisis).

Figure 2.4. Understanding of the causes of climate change, by educational attainment

Percentage of adults selecting 'human activity' as the main cause of climate change, by educational attainment (25-64-year-olds)

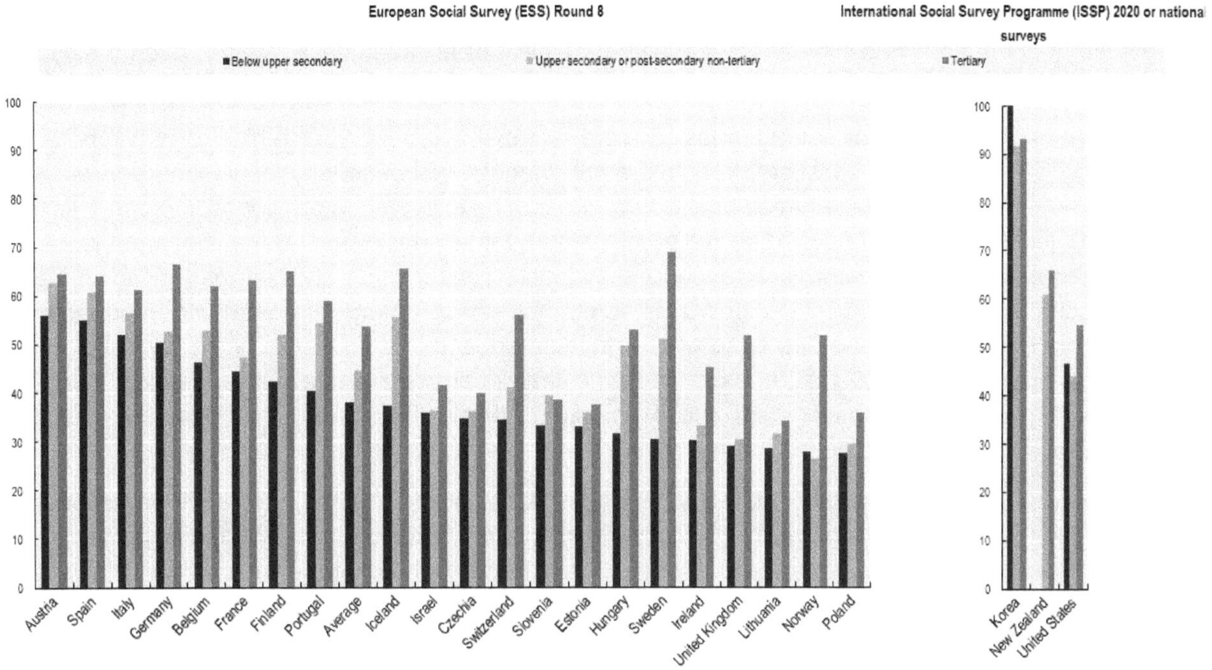

Note: For ESS, the graph shows the proportion of adults who answered the question "Do you think that climate change is caused by natural processes, human activity, or both?" by selecting "mainly by human activity" or "entirely by human activity." For ISSP (Korea, New Zealand and United States), the graph shows the proportion of adults who answered the question "Which of the following statements comes closest to your opinion?" by selecting the statement "The world's climate has been changing mostly due to human activity". For more information see Education at a Glance 2024 Sources, Methodologies and Technical Notes (https://doi.org/10.1787/e7d20315-en).
Source: (OECD, 2024[34]) Education at a Glance 2024: OECD Indicators, OECD Publishing, Paris, https://doi.org/10.1787/c00cad36-en.

There are also indications of widespread misconceptions in the adult population about the impact of different behavioural responses on climate change. In a 2021 international survey of over 21 000 individuals in 30 jurisdictions, the majority of respondents were unable to distinguish high-impact actions from low-impact actions (Ipsos, 2021[36]). For example, 59% of those surveyed believed recycling was among the best ways to reduce their carbon footprint while it was in fact one of the lowest-impact actions proposed in the survey. On average, participants almost consistently ranked low-impact actions such as switching to low-energy lightbulbs as more effective ways to reduce emissions than high-impact actions such as reducing air travel or shifting to a plant-based diet.

Attitudes and action

Attitudes towards environmental and sustainability issues encompass the emotions and beliefs moderated by an individual's value system, shaping their stance on socio-ecological matters and how, when and by whom they should be addressed. Action in response to environmental issues means the outward expression of an individual's attitudes through their behaviours in addressing environmental challenges.

For 15-year-olds, data from PISA 2018 data indicates that pro-environmental attitudes are widespread, with on average nearly 80% of students reporting that caring for the environment is important to them. In some countries, this share rises to 90% of students. No country or economy had less than two-thirds of its student population reporting that caring for the environment was important to them (OECD, 2022[19]). Again, however, socio-economic gaps can be observed, with more advantaged students reporting more pro-environmental attitudes.

Limited information is available on the extent to which these widespread pro-environmental attitudes translate into pro-environmental consumption and lifestyle choices among youth. The PISA 2018 survey asked students about the extent to which they engaged in the following two consumer behaviours: reducing energy use at home and choosing certain products for ethical or environmental reasons even if they are more expensive, with respectively 67% and 44% of students reporting that they did this (Figure 2.5).

Compared to saving energy at home, choosing more expensive products for ethical or environmental reasons may be less popular because it requires more financial resources as well as time and effort in terms of seeking out relevant information on products. As can be expected, a greater socio-economic gap is also observed for choosing more expensive products than for saving energy, with advantaged students being 11 percentage points more likely engage sustainable consumption choices than disadvantaged students (compared to a 6-percentage points difference for saving energy at home). No information is available from PISA 2018 on the degree to which students engage in the lifestyle and daily behavioural choices that are most impactful in terms of reducing individual greenhouse gas emissions, such as changing diets, modes of transportation and consumption levels (see Section on The role of socio-behavioural change in addressing the climate crisis).

Regarding civic action and engagement, PISA 2018 does not offer any specific information on the degree to which students organise or engage in high-visibility action such as strikes, protests and litigation[4]. But it provides some insights into other forms of student activism, namely whether they participate in activities in favour of environmental protection, boycott products or companies for political, ethical or environmental reasons or sign environmental or social petitions online (Figure 2.5). On average across participating countries/economies, some 44% of students report participating in environmental protection activities, and only a bit over a quarter of students report signing petitions online or boycotting products respectively (OECD, 2022[19]).

The very low percentages of students engaging with petitions or boycotts may reflect that these types of actions are not widely perceived by students as effective in addressing environmental challenges. OECD (2022[19]) also highlights that there are cultural differences regarding the social acceptability of these types of actions. However, the surprisingly low percentage of students reporting that they engage in the seemingly catch-all category of "environmental protection activities" likely reflects the existence of other barriers, such as perceived cost, effort, time commitment or public exposure. It is striking that even among the students who are "environmentally enthusiastic"[5], almost 50% convey that they do not engage in any activities to protect the environment (OECD, PISA 2018 Database, Tables B.4.32 and B.4.38).

Figure 2.5. Self-reported student involvement in specific environmental actions

Percentage of 15-year-old students who reported that they were involved in environmental actions

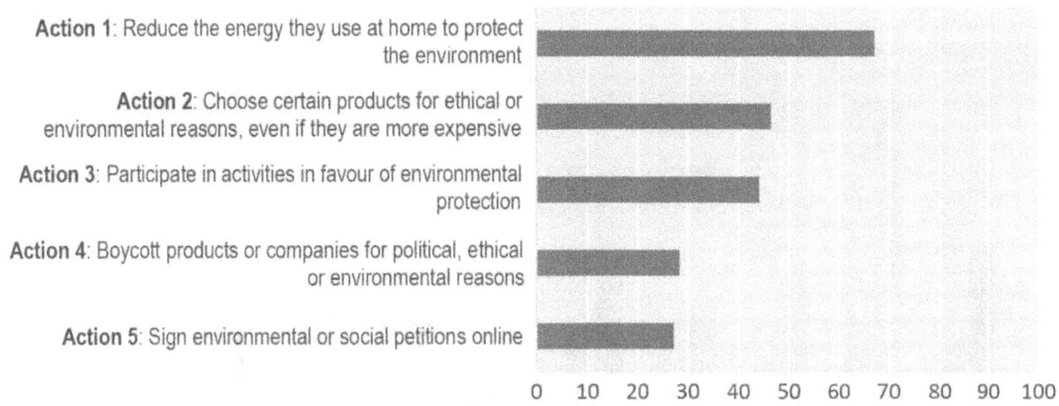

Source: (OECD, 2022[19]) *Are Students Ready to Take on Environmental Challenges?*, PISA, OECD Publishing, Paris, https://doi.org/10.1787/8abe655c-en, https://stat.link/cqxuhm

Data from the OECD's Survey of Social and Emotional Skills (SSES) Round 1 (2019)[6] offers some interesting nuance to these findings on students' environmental action, as the data allow to compare student reports on their environmental action for two different age groups: 10-year-olds and 15-year-olds (Figure 2.6). SSES asked students whether they participated in environmental protection activities outside of school, offering a list of examples, namely recycling, planting a garden/trees and cleaning up trash from an area. While this type of activities have little impact on emissions compared to high-impact behavioural change or collective action and advocacy (see Section on The role of socio-behavioural change in addressing the climate crisis), they may reflect pro-environmental attitudes and dispositions also underlying more impactful action. In all the participating cities, considerably higher shares of 10-year-olds reported participating in environmental protection outside school than 15-year-olds. On average across the participating cities, 50% of 10-year-olds reported that they participated in such activities, compared to only 24% of 15-year-olds (OECD, 2019[37]) .

Figure 2.6. Percentage of 10- and 15-year-old students who participated in environmental protection activities outside of school

Activities included e.g. recycling, planting a garden/trees, cleaning up trash from an area

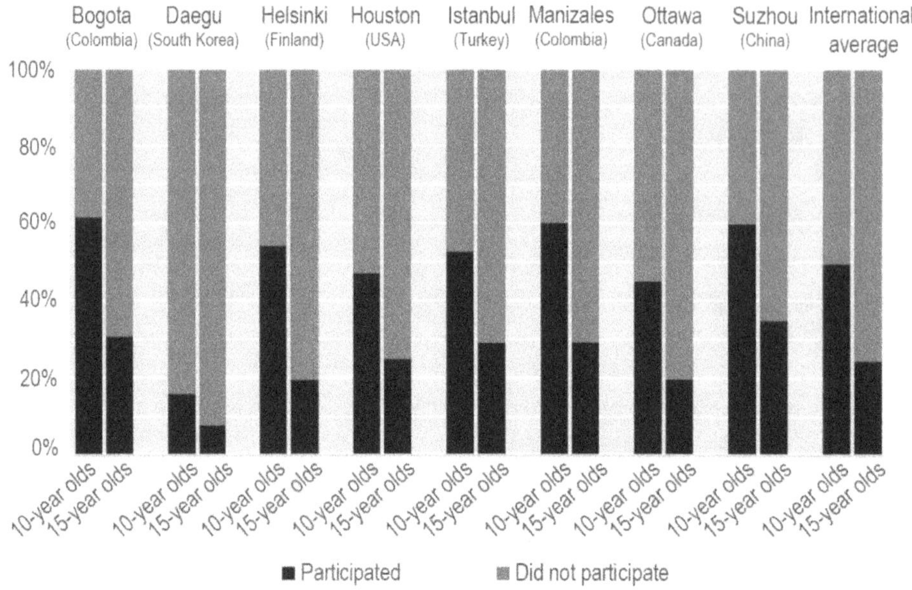

Source: (OECD, 2019[37]) SSES Round 1 Database, https://www.oecd.org/en/data/datasets/SSES-Round-1-Database.html (accessed on 6 December 2024).

These findings are consistent with various academic studies reporting that interest in and concern for the environment evolve with age, with levels of connectedness to nature and willingness to act typically declining from childhood to adolescence, and then rising again in young adults (Pereira and Freire, 2021[14]; Chawla, 2022[38]; Price et al., 2022[39]). This adolescent dip in pro-environmental attitudes and actions points to the need to tailor strategies carefully to the needs and interests of different age groups, in particular the importance of offering environmental and sustainability education for secondary school students at adequate levels of complexity (Nusche, Fuster Rabella and Lauterbach, 2024[13]) (see also Section on Conclusions and policy options).

For adults, data from the *Earth for all survey 2024* (Earth4All, 2024[33]) offers information on societal attitudes to global action on climate change in G20 countries. The results show that on average across G20 countries, 71% of surveyed adults believe that the world must take immediate action within the next decade to reduce emissions from electricity, transport, food, industry, and buildings (Figure 2.7). This indicates that addressing the climate crisis urgently within the current decade is important to a clear majority of adults across G20 countries. This contrasts with the considerably lower levels of understanding regarding the causes of climate change shown in Figure 2.4 for European countries. This difference could indicate a shift in understanding over time, as the ESS data is from 2016, while the data in Figure 2.7 is from 2024. Alternatively, it may reflect higher awareness levels when countries outside of Europe are included in the analysis.

Other factors also influence the degree to which individuals prioritise environmental concerns. Based on analyses of various data sources, Asai et al. (2022[35]) find that people's economic vulnerability and the sectors they work in influence their attitudes towards their environment and support for public policy. For example, individuals who work in the most CO_2-emitting sectors tend to be less worried about climate change than those working in the least CO_2-emitting sectors. Asai et al. (2022[35]) also find that exposure to natural disasters influences environmental attitudes, with individuals being more willing to prioritise the environment when they perceive higher risk of being affected by climate disasters.

Figure 2.7. Attitudes towards global action on climate change

Proportion of adults (18-75 years old) expressing how quickly they think the world should take major action to reduce emissions

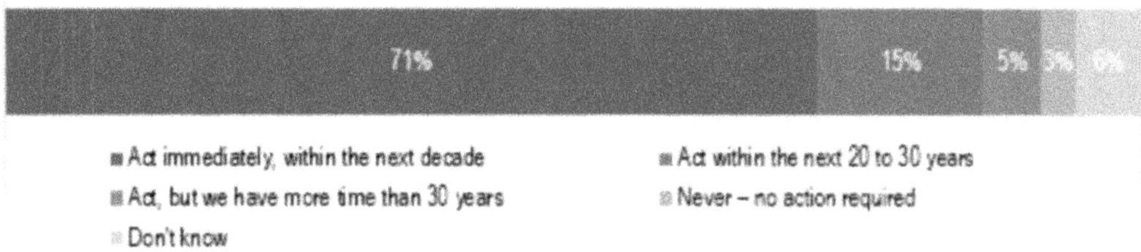

Note: Proportion of adults (18-75 years old) answering the question: "Thinking about climate change and protecting nature, how quickly do you think the world needs to take major action to reduce carbon emissions from electricity, transport, food, industry, and buildings?"
Ipsos surveyed 22,000 participants aged 18 to 55-75 in total across 22 countries (1,000 per country). This included 18 G20 countries (Argentina, Australia, Brazil, Canada, China, France, Germany, India, Indonesia, Italy, Japan, Mexico, Saudi Arabia, South Africa, South Korea, Turkey, United Kingdom, United States), plus four counties outside the G20 (Austria, Denmark, Kenya and Sweden). Not all questions were asked in China. All interviews were conducted online and took place between 5th March and 8th April 2024.
Source: (Earth4All, 2024[33]) *The Earth for All 2024 Survey: Exploring global attitudes to political and economic transformation*, https://earth4all.life/global-survey-2024/. (accessed on 6 December 2024).

While there is widespread agreement among adults in G20 countries that "the world" should take action, other data indicate that the degree to which individuals feel a *personal* responsibility for taking action is more varied. Data from the ESS Round 8 (2016), and from the ISSP (2020) in the case of the United States, indicate that adults from participating nations display varying levels of personal responsibility to contribute to mitigating climate change. On a scale between 0 (indicating no sense of responsibility) and 10 (indicating the strongest sense of responsibility), adults in France and Switzerland reported the highest scores, while those in Czechia, Estonia and Hungary report the lowest (Figure 2.8). On average across all countries surveyed, the score for 25–64-year-olds across OECD countries is 5.9 (Ibid).

Individuals with tertiary education degrees are more likely than those with lower levels of educational attainment to report a strong sense of personal responsibility for contributing to mitigation efforts (OECD, 2024[34]). However, the difference in responsibility across different educational attainment levels seems less striking than the difference observed in environmental awareness (Figure 2.4), with less than a 2-point gap between individuals with below upper secondary education and those with tertiary education on a scale from 1 to 10 (Figure 2.8).

Figure 2.8. Self-reported scores on adults' sense of personal responsibility towards reducing climate change, by educational attainment

Average scores on a scale from 0 to 10, 25-to-64-year-olds

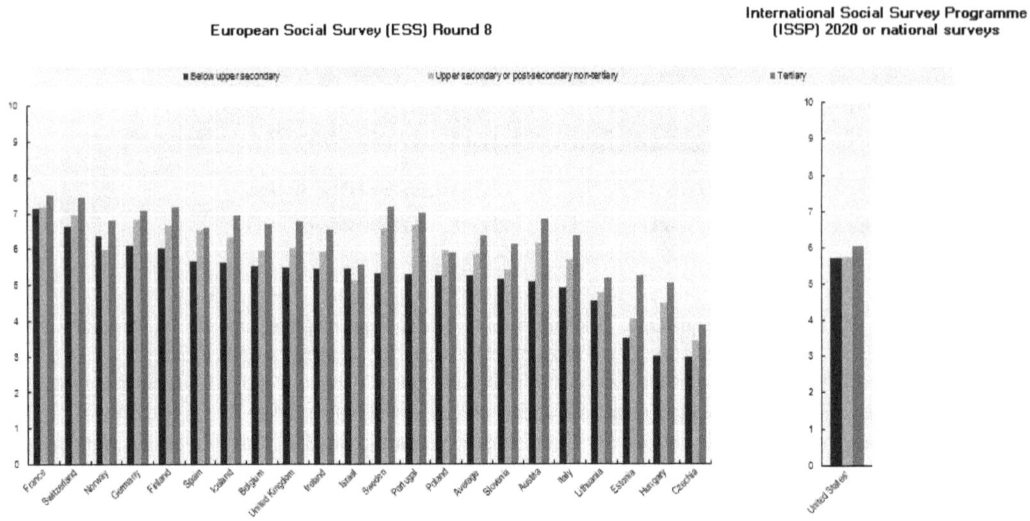

Note: Scores range from 0 to 10, with 0 indicating a complete lack of responsibility towards reducing climate change.
1. Year of reference differs from 2016. Survey question also differs from that used in ESS.
Countries are ranked in descending order of the mean score among adults with below upper secondary educational attainment.
See Table A6.3 (OECD, 2024[34]) for data and for more information see *Education at a Glance 2024 Sources, Methodologies and Technical Notes* (https://doi.org/10.1787/e7d20315-en).
Source: (OECD, 2024[34]) Education at a Glance 2024: OECD Indicators, OECD Publishing, Paris, https://doi.org/10.1787/c00cad36-en.

These findings are corroborated by results from the OECD Survey on Environmental Policies and Individual Behaviour Change (EPIC) 2022 (Box 2.2), which also finds that the share of individuals who consider climate change or other environmental issues to be personally important is higher among those with tertiary educational attainment than those with lower attainment levels (OECD, 2024[34]). In addition, the EPIC Survey offers in-depth insights into household behaviours related to energy use, transportation, waste management, and food consumption (Box 2.2), and the dataset allows disaggregating the responses by educational attainment, which is done for selected indicators below (OECD, 2023[32]).

Box 2.2. Analysis of the OECD Environmental Policies and Individual Behaviour Change (EPIC) survey 2022 household data

The EPIC Survey examines the factors influencing household decisions and the potential effects of policies on these decisions. Conducted in 2022, the survey was carried out in nine countries: Belgium, Canada, France, Israel, the Netherlands, Sweden, Switzerland, the United Kingdom, and the United States. It gathers data on attitudes and behaviours related to energy use, transportation, waste management, and food consumption. Additionally, it includes information on the socio-economic characteristics of respondents, including on their educational attainment levels and households. This comprehensive dataset, encompassing over 17,000 respondents, offers unique insights into attitudes towards the environment, current actions and barriers to adopting more sustainable practices, several of which are highlighted below:

- Energy: The adoption of renewable energy and low-emission technologies remains limited, even when these options are accessible. Among households with the capability to install such equipment, less than one-third have installed heat pumps (30%), solar panels (29%), or battery storage (27%). Uptake is especially low for technologies that involve high initial installation costs or are not well understood.
- Transport: there is a significant dependence on private cars in both rural and urban areas, indicating that electrifying the transport system could be a crucial strategy for reducing emissions in this sector. However, over half (54%) of respondents that regularly use a car report that enhanced public transportation—such as more affordable, frequent, and widespread services—would motivate them to reduce their car usage.
- Food consumption: Affordability (64%), taste (61%), freshness (60%), and nutritional value (54%) are the primary considerations for respondents when purchasing food. The environmental impact of food products is less of a priority, even for those who express environmental concerns.
- Waste practices: Households take steps to reduce waste through low-effort activities like using reusable shopping bags (83%), but struggle to change consumption habits more fundamentally, with fewer buying second-hand items (37%) or renting instead of buying (20%). Those with recycling services produce 26% to 42% less non-recyclable waste, and those charged for waste disposal compost 55% of their food waste compared to 35% among those not charged.

Source: (OECD, 2023[32]) How Green is Household Behaviour?: Sustainable Choices in a Time of Interlocking Crises, OECD Studies on Environmental Policy and Household Behaviour, OECD Publishing, Paris, https://doi.org/10.1787/2bbbb663-en.

Figure 2.9 depicts the proportion of adults expressing their willingness to reduce car use if public transport systems were improved, by educational attainment. The figure shows that across all surveyed countries, individuals with tertiary education consistently report a higher willingness to switch to public transport compared to those with non-tertiary education, suggesting that higher education levels are associated with a tendency to prioritise environmental and climate considerations over other considerations such as (perceived or actual) comfort and safety.

Figure 2.9. Willingness to reduce car use

Percentage of adults (25-54 years old) expressing a willingness to reduce car use with improved public transport services, by educational attainment

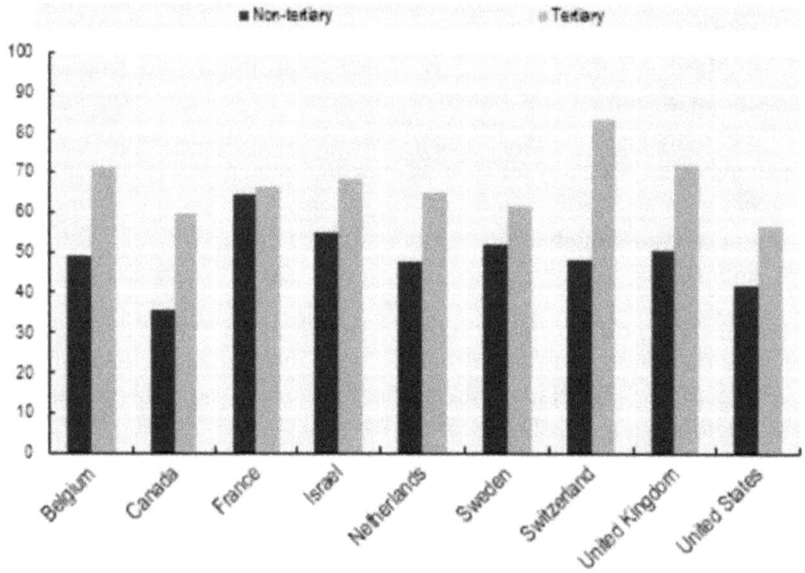

Note: Proportion of adults (25-54 years old) who responded positively to the questions "Would better public transport services (e.g. more frequent, more accessible, etc.) lead you to use a car less?"
Source: Based on data from the 2022 OECD Survey on Environmental Policy and Individual Behaviour Change (EPIC) in (OECD, 2023[32]) *How Green is Household Behaviour? Sustainable Choices in a Time of Interlocking Crises*, OECD Studies on Environmental Policy and Household Behaviour, https://doi.org/10.1787/2bbbb663-en.

Figure 2.10 offers additional insights on the criteria that adults consider when purchasing food. As reported in Box 2.2, overall, consumers consider the environmental impact of food products less important than other criteria such as affordability (64%), taste (61%), freshness (60%), and nutritional value (54%). However, when looking at the minority of respondents who did respond that environmental concerns were a priority when purchasing food, an interesting pattern emerges regarding the specific environmental concerns that they consider. On average across countries, the relatively abstract consideration of reducing emissions that contribute to climate change is considered least important, compared with more tangible considerations such as organic and local production, animal welfare and minimal packaging.

Figure 2.10 also shows that individuals who consider the environmental impacts of food production are predominantly those with tertiary education. While this pattern might indicate an important role played by tertiary education in shaping consumer choices, it is important to note that some of these environmentally-conscious choices (e.g. the choice for organic and locally-produced food) are also often linked to purchasing power. People with higher incomes, who more frequently have higher educational attainment, can afford to make choices that are less driven by cost. Indeed, EPIC finds that, among all factors considered when purchasing food, respondents with higher incomes are more likely to prioritise environmental considerations compared to those with lower incomes (OECD, 2023[32]). This interplay between education and socio-economic status must also be considered when examining consumer behaviour towards more sustainable practices.

Figure 2.10. Priorities when making food purchases by educational attainment

Percentage of respondents prioritising various environmental considerations by educational attainment, adults (25-54 years old)

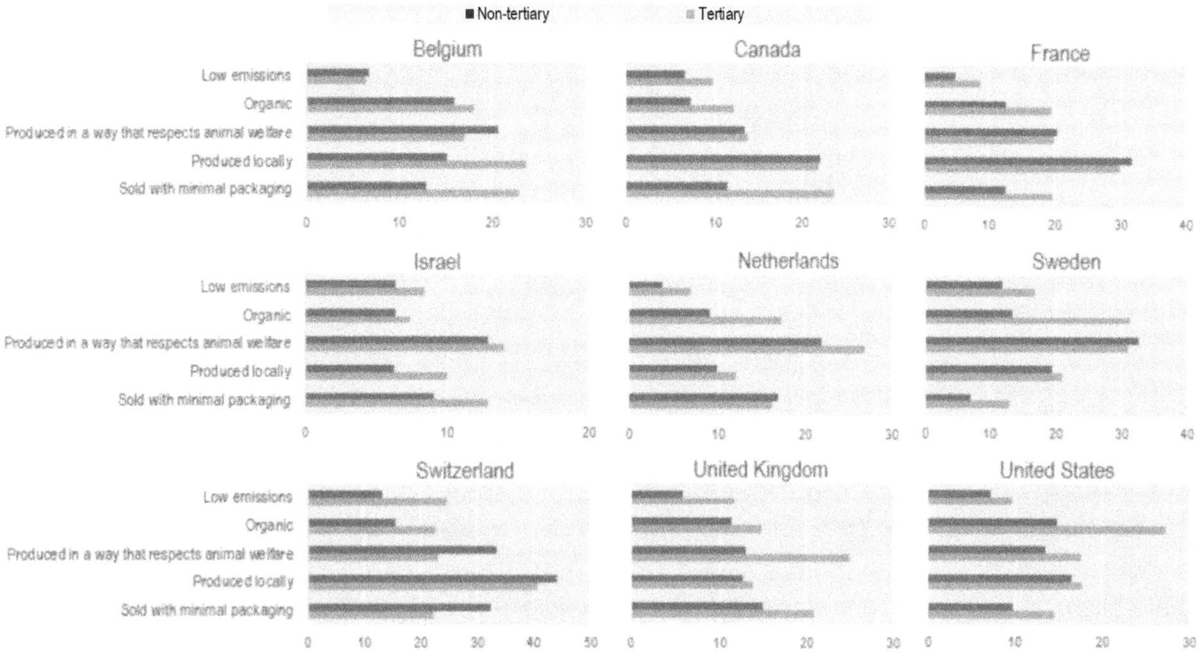

Note: Survey participants were presented with the following question: "What is most important to you when you are choosing which foods to buy? Please select up to five of the following: It is easy to prepare; It tastes good, It is healthy; It emits relatively few emissions that contribute to climate change; It is affordable; It can be easily bought or is widely accessible; It is made and sold by people who have good working conditions; It is produced in a way that respects animal welfare; It is organic; It is unprocessed; It is produced locally; It is sold with minimal packaging; It is not easily perishable; It is fresh." For respondents in each educational attainment category, the figure shows the percentage indicating that they prioritise attributes that could be perceived as environmentally relevant (namely: Low emissions, Organic, Produced in a way that respects animal welfare, Produced locally and Sold with minimal packaging). While concern for animal welfare is not a direct environmental concern, it is often aligned with sustainable farming and production methods, which benefit the environment. Humane practices reduce pollution, enhance biodiversity, improve soil health, and reduce resource consumption and GHG emissions, supporting broader environmental goals and contributing to overall sustainability.

Source: Based on data from the 2022 OECD Survey on Environmental Policy and Individual Behaviour Change (EPIC) in (OECD, 2023[32]), How Green is Household Behaviour?: Sustainable Choices in a Time of Interlocking Crises, OECD Studies on Environmental Policy and Household Behaviour, https://doi.org/10.1787/2bbbb663-en.

When it comes to indicators of civic and public engagement of the general population, there has been a notable shift in societal attitudes and behaviours towards climate change, reflecting a growing awareness and engagement with environmental issues. This shift is evidenced by the increasing visibility of climate concerns in public discourse, the rise of grassroots movements, and a broader acceptance of sustainable practices across various sectors of society.

In recent years, climate change has become a central issue in political discourse and public debate, fostering the potential for the adoption of more ambitious policies and the removal of existing barriers. The growing coverage in newspapers and on television reflects the increasing public dissemination of information about climate change, making it accessible to a broader audience. As shown in Figure 2.11, media coverage of climate change has steadily increased since 2015, with fluctuations often tied to significant events or geopolitical developments (Roeser et al., 2023[17]; Aoyagi et al., 2024[40]) This trend highlights how climate change has progressively entered the mainstream, particularly following the adoption of the Paris Agreement, which has contributed to a heightened global awareness of the issue.

Figure 2.11. Media coverage of climate change or global warming

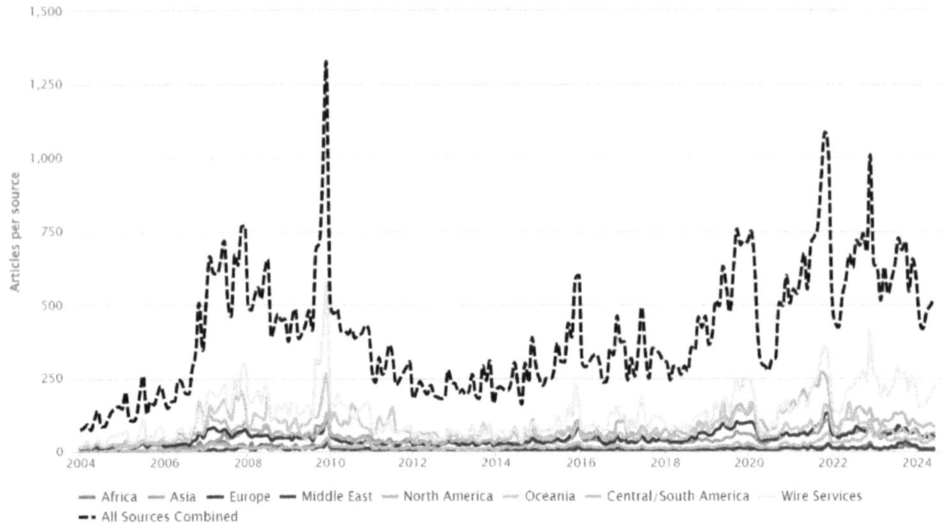

Note: Different peaks correspond to different events as for example the all-time high 2010 peak following UNCCC COP in Copenhagen.
Source: (Aoyagi et al., 2024[40]), *World Newspaper Coverage of Climate Change or Global Warming, 2004-2024*, https://sciencepolicy.colorado.edu/icecaps/research/media_coverage/world/index.html (accessed on 5 December 2024).

There has been a global rise in significant climate movements, such as the notable Fridays for Future, driven by increasing youth engagement with environmental issues. For example, in 2019, environment-related protests in the United States more than doubled compared to 2018, with a 404% increase in March and an extraordinary 845% surge during the global climate strike in September (Brannen, Haig and Schmidt, 2020[41]).While climate protests have predominantly occurred in Europe and the United States, they are not limited to these countries, and Fridays for Future has reported demonstrations in 177 countries across all continents.

Climate protests between 2016 and 2021 have been shown to lead to an increase in media coverage of the issue (Lochner, Stechemesser and Wenz, 2024[42]) and to an increase in concern among the general population (Brehm and Gruhl, 2024[43]). In Germany, Valentim (2023[44]) shows that exposure to Friday for Futures protests boosts the Green Party's vote share, with repeated exposure to these demonstrations amplifying the effect further. In Switzerland, the Fridays for Future (FFF) movement has been widely perceived positively by the Swiss public, with nearly one-third of participants in a survey reporting increased environmental awareness and behaviour changes, particularly in private behaviours such as mobility and consumption (Fritz et al., 2023[45]). In addition, in the United States context, it has been demonstrated that peaceful marches increase support for the climate movement among independents and Democrats (Khatibi et al., 2021[10]). Civil disobedience positively affects only Democrats, with no observed effects among Republicans and no "backfire" effects for any group, highlighting the effectiveness of tactical diversity and the interaction between partisanship and protest in shaping movement support (Ibid).

Alongside the rise of the climate movement, there has been a surge of so-called “anti-climate” protests. Figure 2.12 shows aggregate attendance at climate-related protests worldwide since 2022, capturing the post-COVID recovery in civic mobilization. The figure reveals that larger anti-climate protests particularly gained momentum in the third quarter of 2022 and the first quarter of 2024 – the only periods where attendance at anti-climate protests exceeded that of pro-climate movements, with over 70,000 participants during these times. Despite receiving considerable media attention, these surges remain significantly lower than the pro-climate protests, which amassed over one million participants in the first and third quarters of 2023.

Figure 2.12. Attendance to protests relating to climate policy around the world since 2022

Aggregate participation (in number of participants) in climate-related protests around the world

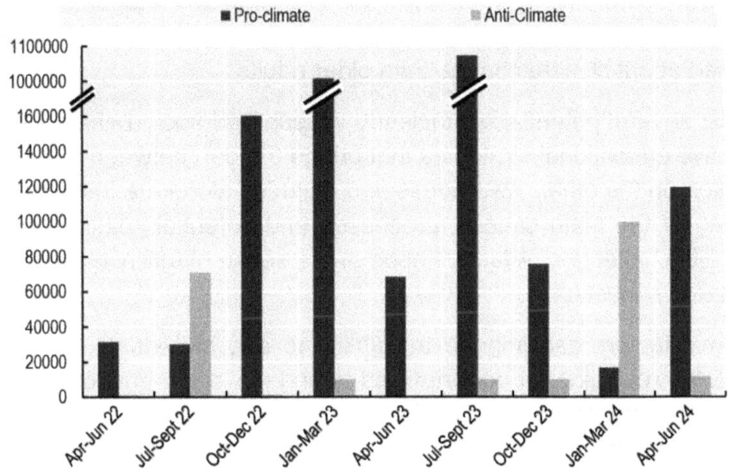

Note: The figure aggregates pro- and anti-climate protests since 2022, reflecting the post-COVID recovery period in civic mobilization, using attendance data from Carnegie's Climate Protest Tracker. Protests range from demands for stronger climate action to opposition against existing policies, with outcomes such as policy shifts or corporate commitments. The data relies on peak protest attendance estimates, which can vary as local authorities often underestimate crowd sizes, while organizers may overestimate them, and presents therefore best estimates. The tracker focuses on mass climate-related protests, excluding many smaller-scale mobilizations that may not have gained significant attention, especially in non-English media. As a result, the figure reflects major episodes of climate activism, primarily reported in English, with additional data from French and Mandarin sources, capturing key post-pandemic trends in global climate activism.
Source: Adapted from (Carnegie, n.d.[46]) Carnegie Endowment for International Peace's Climate Protest Tracker, https://carnegieendowment.org/features/climate-protest-tracker?lang=en (accessed on 5 December 2024).

Anti-climate movements are diverse, encompassing a degree of climate scepticism but also often driven by other concerns, such as opposition to policies perceived as unjust or poorly implemented. The *Mouvement des Gilets jaunes* [Yellow Vest movement] in France, for example, was not explicitly anti-climate but protested against a proposed carbon tax that was seen as disproportionately burdening lower-income groups (Mehleb, Kallis and Zografos, 2021[47]). This illustrates that much of the resistance in that movement was not against climate action itself but rather the way these policies were implemented. Recent analysis of the current surge anti-climate movement in Europe also emphasises that opposition emerges when policies are viewed as unfair or lacking transparency (Youngs, 2024[48]). This suggests that although the climate backlash may intuitively be seen as a counter-movement or a regression in response to the rise of pro-climate activism, it is, in fact, more complex. The politics surrounding the green transition have become a central issue within democratic processes, reflecting not necessarily a weakening of the climate movement, but rather an increasing complexity in addressing societal concerns regarding the equity and implementation of climate policies. This complexity deserves careful attention to avoid deepening polarisation and to ensure the green transition is both inclusive and just.

Emerging agency and equity concerns

The analysis in the previous section reveals various connections between awareness, attitudes and actions with respect to environmental, sustainability and climate challenges. However, there are some inconsistencies in these relationships: while a large majority of individuals report high levels of awareness and concern, a smaller proportion feels personal responsibility for contributing to climate change mitigation, and an even smaller share actually engages in pro-environmental actions.

The analysis also shows that awareness, attitudes and actions are influenced by educational attainment and socio-economic backgrounds, which are often interrelated, as individuals from more privileged backgrounds more frequently complete higher levels of education. In addition, the lifecycle perspective revealed interesting age differences, with younger (10-year-old) students more engaged in pro-environmental activities than older (15-year-old) students, and younger adults more knowledgeable/informed about climate change than older adults.

These findings suggest several potential obstacles to widespread socio-behavioural change. First, there may be a lack of effective educational strategies that bridge the gap between awareness and attitudes on the one hand, and action on the other. Awareness and attitudes alone are insufficient if individuals do not have full understanding of the main causes, processes and potential solutions with respect to climate change and sustainability challenges. A lack of hope and a sense of futility may further reduce motivation for change and contribute to inaction.

Second, socio-economic factors can impede the ability to act; individuals from lower socio-economic backgrounds may lack the resources or opportunities to engage in pro-environmental behaviours despite their awareness and/or pro-environmental attitudes. In addition, social and cultural factors might also play a role, where societal norms and peer influences either support or hinder pro-environmental actions. This is of particular concern considering that more privileged groups generally have larger carbon footprints than less privileged groups (Box 2.3).

This highlights the complexity of translating environmental awareness into action, underscoring the need for targeted educational and policy interventions. Several fundamental questions arise:

- While awareness of environmental and climate challenges is high across OECD and partner countries, understanding of their causes, consequences and potential solutions is much more variable. How can education ensure that all learners leave compulsory education with adequate understanding of existential socio-ecological risks?
- Even among individuals with strong knowledge outcomes and pro-environmental attitudes, translating these into action faces obstacles. How can education help bridge the gap between caring about sustainability and climate issues and the actual engagement in action?
- Higher levels of education consistently correlate with greater pro-environmental attitudes, potentially removing obstacles to action. Given that collective action and policy acceptance require broad engagement, how can the education sector enhance engagement among the groups who do not pursue post-compulsory education?
- While self-reported environmental awareness, attitudes and actions are higher among socio-economically advantaged groups, more advantaged groups typically have higher carbon footprints than less advantaged groups (see Box 2.3), a fact that is frequently overlooked. How can education highlight this disparity and promote more sustainable practices among all socio-economic groups? How can the education sector ensure a more effective and inclusive approach to environmental action?

The remainder of this chapter proposes a range of policy options to address these questions and provides key leverage points that education systems can focus on to support societies at large in overcoming some of the obstacles they currently face in tackling the climate and other environmental crises.

Box 2.3. Carbon inequality

A stark relationship between wealth and carbon emissions exists, showing that more advantaged groups typically have significantly higher carbon footprints (OXFAM, 2020[49]; Chancel et al., 2022[50]). OXFAM, (2020[49]) presents data highlighting the vast inequality in carbon emissions, with the wealthiest segments of the population disproportionately consuming the world's limited carbon budget. For example, between 1990 and 2015, the wealthiest 10% of the global population, approximately 630 million people, are responsible for a staggering 52% of cumulative carbon emissions, effectively consuming nearly a third (31%) of the global carbon budget for limiting warming to 1.5°C. Within this group, the richest 1% alone—around 63 million individuals—accounted for over 15% of cumulative emissions, using 9% of the carbon budget, which is more than twice the emissions of the poorest 50% of humanity. Meanwhile, the global middle class, comprising 40% of humanity (around 2.5 billion people), contributed 41% of cumulative emissions, using 25% of the carbon budget, while the poorest 50% accounted for just 7% of emissions, depleting a mere 4% of the budget. These disparities are driven primarily by consumption patterns, which include frequent air travel, ownership of large homes and household behaviour, and extensive use of private vehicles.

Chancel et al. (2022[50]) look into the implications of inequalities in the distribution of economic assets, on global ecological inequalities. The study finds that carbon inequalities between regions are large and persistent. For example, in 2019, per capita emissions in Sub-Saharan Africa are 1.6 tonnes per person per year, just a quarter of the global average, while North America has much higher emissions at 21 tonnes per capita, three times the world average. Other regions vary, with South and South-East Asia at 2.6 tonnes per capita and Latin America at 4.8 tonnes, followed by Middle East and North Africa, East Asia, Europe, and Russia and Central Asia, where emissions range between 7.5 and 10 tonnes per capita. Strikingly, carbon inequalities within regions are more pronounced than those between regions, with significant disparities in carbon footprints observed across different income groups in every region. For example, in East Asia, the top 10% emit nearly 40 tonnes of carbon annually compared to around three tonnes by the poorest 50%, while in North America, the top 10% emit over 70 tonnes, and the bottom 50% emit fewer than 10 tonnes.

Given these disparities, it is crucial that education systems address the disconnect between environmental awareness and actual carbon footprints by promoting not only awareness but also actionable, equitable strategies for reducing emissions across all socio-economic groups, with a particular focus on reducing the disproportionately high carbon consumption.

Source: (OXFAM, 2020[49]) *Confronting Carbon Inequality - Putting climate justice at the heart of the COVID-19 recovery*, https://oxfamilibrary.openrepository.com/bitstream/handle/10546/621052/mb-confronting-carbon-inequality-210920-en.pdf (accessed on 30 August 2024); (Chancel et al., 2022[50]), *World Inequality Report 2022*, World Inequality Lab, https://wir2022.wid.world/ (accessed on 9 December 2024).

Conclusions and policy options

Identifying the "sustainability competencies" underlying socio-behavioural change

There is wide agreement that empowering individuals to exercise their agency in the 21st century requires attention to developing a set of transversal competencies that are essential to function in today's fast-changing societies, fractured by multiple global crises. Definition of these key competencies, sometimes called "21st century competencies" vary across countries and contexts, but they typically include strong literacy and numeracy skills; media, information and digital literacy, critical thinking, creativity, collaboration and a growth mindset (OECD, 2019[28]) (OECD, 2021[25]).

In the context of climate change and the green transition, a set of additional competencies and values have been added to the list of key competencies by researchers, and increasingly in curriculum frameworks, aiming to capture ways of being and thinking in the world that may best allow individuals to address sustainability challenges (see Box 2.4 below for some international examples).

While definitions and frameworks vary, there is broad consensus that agency in the context of sustainability challenges builds on transversal scientific thinking and systems thinking skills, but encompasses a broader range of cognitive, affective, socio-emotional and behavioural dimensions. In particular, the complexity of socio-ecological challenges requires attention to the social dimensions of human agency, such as the importance of collaboration with others and respect for diverse perspectives in developing responses to socio-ecological crises. Some key dimensions of agency in the context of socio-ecological challenges are addressed in more detail in the following sub-sections.

Box 2.4. International frameworks articulating sustainability competencies

UNESCO's sustainability competencies were developed in the context of its work on Education for Sustainable Development (ESD). UNESCO developed a guide in 2017 (last updated in 2023) that identifies learning objectives, activities and topics for each of the Sustainable Development Goals. Beyond listing specialised competencies for each of the individual SDGs, the guide describes general key competencies for sustainability. These comprise the following: systems-thinking competency; anticipatory competency; normative competency; strategic competency; collaboration competency; critical thinking competency; self-awareness competency; and integrated problem-solving competence.

The European Commission's GreenComp Framework defines four competency areas and 12 competences for sustainability, applicable to all learners in any setting and age group (Bianchi, Pisiotis and Cabrera Giraldez, 2022[51]). These competencies aim to enable learners to understand and address sustainability challenges in a holistic and transformative way. The four competence areas are:

- ***embodying sustainability values***, which includes valuing sustainability, supporting fairness and promoting nature
- ***embracing complexity in sustainability***, which includes systems thinking, critical thinking and problem framing
- ***envisioning sustainable futures***, which includes futures literacy, adaptability and exploratory thinking
- ***acting for sustainability***, which includes political agency, collective action and individual initiative

The Environmental Sustainability Competence Toolbox is a framework proposed by the OECD and the European Commission, which extends the GreenComp framework to include additional competence areas that are relevant for sustainability and have been defined and assessed as part of the OECD's Programme for International Student Assessment (PISA). The additional competences are presented as crucial for equipping students with a wide range of cognitive, affective and behavioural capabilities that should allow them to play a positive role in shaping the future of the environment. The four areas are the following:

- ***environmental awareness***: students have a baseline of science proficiency and report knowledge of or familiarity with environmental issues and climate change,

- ***sense-of-purpose***: students agree or strongly agree that looking after the environment is important to them,
- ***science self-efficacy***: students report that they can complete tasks with regard to climate change "easily" or "with a bit of effort",
- ***environmental behaviour***: students engage in energy saving or in collective action to protect the environment.

Source: (Nusche, Fuster Rabella and Lauterbach, 2024[13]) "Rethinking Education in the Context of Climate Change: Leverage Points for Transformative Change", OECD Education Working Papers, No. 307, OECD Publishing, Paris, https://doi.org/10.1787/f14c8a81-en.

Building foundational scientific literacy among all learners

As highlighted above, having a solid understanding of the climate challenge is crucial for individuals to make informed decisions to act. Knowing about the basic causes, processes and potential responses to climate change enables individuals to evaluate, critique and transform new information, thereby enhancing their ability to act autonomously and effectively within their contexts. Results from both PISA 2015 and PISA 2018 show that there is a strong correlation between students' performance on the environmental sustainability items and students' performance on the overall PISA science test. The association between performance in environmental sustainability and performance in the general science test is also observed at the system level: countries/economies where the mean score in science is higher tend to perform better on the environmental sustainability test units (OECD, 2022[19]).

While not allowing to infer causality, these findings indicate that the knowledge, concepts and ways of thinking that students acquire when building their *general* scientific literacy are also highly relevant for building *specific* environmental science literacy. Boosting overall science education is therefore likely to be an effective way to build some of the scientific literacy competences needed to understand, analyse and respond effectively to environmental and sustainability questions. Further analysis of PISA 2018 data also shows that higher science performance is strongly associated with awareness of climate change, self-efficacy with respect to climate change knowledge, as well as pro-environmental attitudes (OECD, 2022[19]; OECD, 2023[52]).

At the same time, further analyses have shown that, while important, scientific literacy does not automatically lead to learners to adopt sustainable behaviours, take pro-environmental actions or choose sustainable careers. Other factors, in particular values, worldviews and social contexts are important parts of the decision making in proposing responses to climate challenges and will be addressed below (OECD, 2023[12]; OECD, 2022[19]).

The process of acquiring adequate understanding of socio-ecological challenges should not be misunderstood as a passive process of accumulating knowledge, but as one of acquiring a level of scientific literacy that learners can apply in all subjects as an active and dynamic resource that underpins the exercise of agency in various domains. Foundational scientific knowledge and skills, such as the ability to evaluate different sources of evidence and the understanding that scientific knowledge is conditional and constantly evolving, are essential for individuals to exercise agency effectively. Without these foundational scientific thinking skills, individuals may struggle to overcome obstacles, make strategic choices, and achieve their goals due to a lack of necessary understanding. Box 2.5 provides an example of a project-based initiative aimed at promoting scientific and critical thinking in secondary schools, presenting early results that point to the initiative's effectiveness in fostering these skills among students.

Box 2.5. Scientific thinking for all: A toolkit

Scientists have long developed and refined techniques to mitigate bias and prevent cognitive traps, yet these valuable methods are rarely comprehensively taught in secondary education. To bridge this gap, Nobel Prize laureate Saul Perlmutter, researchers at the University of California Berkeley, and Nobel Prize Outreach have initiated the development of a curriculum titled *Scientific Thinking for All: A Toolkit*. This curriculum aims to equip students with the cognitive tools necessary to navigate complex real-world issues, fostering not only scientific reasoning but also collaborative problem-solving and critical thinking skills across diverse perspectives (Nobel Prize Outreach, 2024[53]).

The full curriculum, set to be completed by 2025, will consist of six units that address 20 fundamental concepts, ranging from causal reasoning to probabilistic thinking and human cognition. The project-based, hands-on approach encourages students to engage with real-world problems, such as decisions around clean water access or transitioning to clean energy. Unit 1, focusing on the iterative nature of scientific evidence through the lens of water quality, and Unit 6, focusing on group decision-making strategies through the lens of energy decisions, are already available (Nobel Prize Outreach, 2024[53]), with pilot phases for other units underway. Designed for continuous improvement, the curriculum leverages iterative feedback from educators, who have reported high levels of student engagement due to the relevance and inquiry-based nature of the content.

Preliminary results from pilot testing indicate substantial improvements in critical thinking skills. Students showed notable progress in understanding science as a dynamic and evolving process, enhanced their ability to reason through uncertainty, and became better at differentiating between facts and values, all after engaging with just one unit of the curriculum. The programme is designed to further strengthen these abilities by revisiting core concepts through various approaches and applications. Beyond equipping students with critical thinking tools, the curriculum seeks to foster a shared understanding of reality, empowering diverse groups to collaboratively solve complex problems—an essential skill for tackling 21st century challenges.

Note: Students demonstrated enhanced abilities in recognising science as a dynamic process (d = .68), reasoning about uncertainty (d = .36), and distinguishing between facts and values (d = .50). d refers to Cohen's d, which is a measure of effect size used in statistics.
Source: Contribution provided by Lawrence Hall of Science, University of California, Berkeley, unpublished results. (Nobel Prize Outreach, 2024[53])

Supporting systems thinking as an essential tool to deal with complexity

Among the competencies that are essential to solving sustainability challenges, systems thinking has recently gained attention as a key higher-order cognitive skill that gives individuals the disposition to understand the complex nature of climate change and to address this complexity when thinking about solutions. Systems thinking can be defined as the ability to understand complex interrelationships, interconnections and feedback loops among the components of a given system (Ben-Zvi-Assaraf and Orion, 2010[54]; Orgill, York and MacKellar, 2019[55]; Voulvoulis et al., 2022[56]).

Systems thinking is based on the understanding that social, economic, ecological and other systems are increasingly complex and interdependent, and that the aggregate phenomena that emerge do so as a reflection of the interaction between all the participants in the system (Hynes, Lees and Müller, 2020[57]). This involves viewing complex phenomena as interconnected and interdependent components within a larger system. It emphasises the relationships, patterns, and dynamics among these components rather than focusing on individual elements in isolation (White et al., 2023[29]).

Systems thinking can significantly empower individuals by demonstrating how their actions contribute to larger systems, thus preventing feelings of futility. When individuals recognise that their actions are part of a broader essential effort towards sustainability and climate resilience, they are more likely to feel motivated and empowered to take meaningful action. By showcasing the ripple effects of personal and collective actions within complex systems, systems thinking can help combat apathy and instil a sense of agency, purpose and efficacy in addressing climate challenges.

A systems-thinking approach emphasises the importance of adaptability and responsiveness in individual actions, policy, and decision-making. It acknowledges that the complex, interconnected nature of systems requires continuous learning and adjustment. This perspective aligns with contemporary understandings of policy making in the face of major crises, where high levels of uncertainty demand flexible and adaptive approaches, often referred to as "decision-making under uncertainty" (Lempert, 2019[58]; Haasnoot et al., 2013[59]). Learners who understand the dynamic nature of these problems and the corresponding responses are better equipped to engage civically with public policy. This understanding fosters a more informed and proactive community capable of contributing to policy development and implementation in ways that are responsive to real-time changes and uncertainties.

In addition, systems thinking recognises that systems are constantly evolving and are neither in nor converging towards a steady state, meaning that forecasting cannot rely on extrapolations from the past or on the analysis of isolated individual part of the system behaviour (Hynes, Lees and Müller, 2020[57]). Instead, it requires an understanding of the dynamic interactions within the system, which can lead to unexpected and non-linear outcomes. This understanding can empower learners of all ages by showing that the future is not predetermined to follow the same path of the past, thereby fostering a sense of hope and encouraging innovative thinking.

Analysis shows that there is a sharp increase in the number of systems thinking studies in the field of education research since 2016 (Bielik et al., 2023[60]). However, most of these studies focus on higher education, followed by high school and less on elementary students (Ibid). Enhancing the ability of students of all ages to become system thinkers requires an enhanced ability of teachers, at different stages of students' lives, to apply fit-for-purpose methods, training and programs effectively.

Approaches for fostering system thinking may vary significantly according to the age of the students. For younger students, such as 4th graders, hands-on, inquiry-based learning that includes outdoor activities and lab experiments can be highly effective in helping them recognise and analyse system components and interconnections in real-world contexts (Assaraf and Orion, 2009[61]). In contrast, older students, such as those in secondary school, can also benefit more from structured digital courses that incorporate lessons, videos, and cognitive tasks designed to enhance their ability to analyse complex systems and understand relationships within them (Al-Menshawi and Abu Al-Yazeed, 2020[62]). Box 2.6 illustrates an initiative which aims to tailor learning to the needs of adolescents in secondary schools worldwide, by offering a systems-based educational framework that deepens understanding of climate complexity and fosters active participation.

Box 2.6. The Climate Academy: The rewards of engaging in complexity

The Climate Academy is a climate education programme currently engaging students in eight countries including from India, Luxembourg, Belgium and the United States. As environmental engagement tends to decline from early childhood, reaching its lowest point in early adolescence before stabilising in adulthood (Section on Fostering behavioural and social change for a sustainable future: a lifelong learning approach), the Climate Academy developed an approach targeted specifically at students in secondary education. While the reasons for the adolescent dip in environmental engagement are not fully understood, the Climate Academy proposes that a key factor may be the lack of complexity in environmental education. As other subjects advance in depth and complexity, environmental education often remains fragmented and repetitive, lacking the integrated framework necessary to engage adolescents who seek deeper, systemic understanding of global issues.

To address this gap, the Climate Academy aims to enhance climate education through a systems-informed approach designed to engage students aged 15-18 years old in the complexity of climate issues (The Climate Academy, n.d.[63]). The Academy has developed its own pedagogical material, offering concise yet in-depth content that promotes learning across various dimensions of the climate challenge and actionable responses, structured around three core pillars. The first pillar, Systems Understanding, equips students with a comprehensive view of climate change as a systemic issue, moving beyond individual actions to grasp the crisis' interconnected complexities. This is developed through a 16-step course that deepens both environmental and human understanding. The second pillar, Civic Service, engages students in translating their learning into impactful projects and initiatives, fostering community involvement and building leadership skills through peer teaching and public speaking. The third pillar, Systems Entrepreneurship, encourages students to tackle systemic barriers and propose innovative solutions for societal change, empowering them with resilience and the tools to shape sustainable futures. Students are rewarded with a range of certificates that recognise deeper competences in Systems Understanding, Civic Engagement and Systems Entrepreneurship.

In 2024, the programme operated in eight countries and mobilised roughly 750 students in these countries, ranging from climate enthusiasts but also students with lesser environmental interest, who have a motivation to prove their high-level credentials for university applications or jobs. In March 2025, the Academy will award over 600 Bronze certificates in Systems Understanding to students across India who will have completed the 16 steps. These students will also receive different levels of certification in Civic Service after brining this understanding into the public space through publications and events. One of the Climate Academy's notable projects, "The Writings on the Wall," helps students translate complex scientific concepts into public engagement through artistic means, such as murals at cultural festivals that had thousands of participants. Fifteen students from the Academy in Brussels will receive Gold certificates in recognition of their 'Deep Green Travel' event to Varese in Italy: travelling by train, eating vegan, and using their week in the city to run workshops in schools, organise an event in a university, launch an art competition about climate systems collapse and how it disproportionately impacts women, and interview people in the street about climate literacy as an evidence base for an published article. Through this programme, the Climate Academy aims to fill an educational gap by providing the complexity and depth needed for active participation in climate solutions and discussions.

Source: (Seleviciute and Sturlyte, 2021[64]) *With Art Protest, Concerned Students Raise Climate Alarm*, https://news-decoder.com/with-art-protest-concerned-students-raise-climate-alarm/ (accessed on 5 December 2024); (VIBGYOR Group of Schools, 2024[65]), https://www.instagram.com/reel/C5lOm5cPIU4/?igsh=MW53amhtZTA0a3FyNw%3D%3D (accessed on 5 December 2024).
(The Climate Academy, n.d.[63]), *The Climate Academy*, https://theclimateacademy.org/ (accessed on 17 September 2024).

Fostering individual and collective action capacity via experiential learning

Equipping learners with understanding of the intricate relationships between ecological and human systems and the cognitive skills to identify effective solutions can contribute to building a sense of agency, self-efficacy and commitment to contributing to sustainability. Yet, a disproportionate focus on individual action may lead to a sense of futility, isolation and low subjective well-being. By contrast, social trust, support and a sense of collective action are key to effective action strategies (Ojala, 2016[66]).

Research indicates that experiential and project-based learning is of particular importance in supporting students' individual and collective action competencies. In this context, whole-school approaches and place-based education approaches (PBE), *i.e.* those that are locally driven, community based, or ecologically focused can offer an adequate setting to connect learning to experiences. PBE approaches may include outdoor, community- and service-learning, which all seek to engage students cognitively, emotionally and physically in their learning while fostering a sense of connection between them and their surroundings (Elfer, 2011[67]).

Such approaches are found to encourage students to "make connections between content areas" (Foster and Piacentini, 2023[68]) and engage competencies such as critical thinking, creativity, collaboration and problem-solving (Hargreaves, 2008[69]; Tilbury and Galvin, 2022[70]). A companion paper to this report (Nusche, Fuster Rabella and Lauterbach, 2024[13]) offers a comprehensive review of PBE approaches in school education, how they can foster practical and authentic learning and engagement, as well as some of the challenges around this type of learning (Box 2.7).

Box 2.7. Place-based education to foster agency, equity and inclusion in learning about sustainability

Case studies exemplify that PBE can positively impact cognitive, emotional, and environmental outcomes across education levels when tailored to students' developmental stages (Hernandez Gonzalez, 2023[71]). A central idea in PBE theory is that such a direct experience of sustainability concepts in specific places not only facilitates understanding, but also positive emotions like a sense of connectedness, belonging and care towards these places (Schweizer, Davis and Thompson, 2013[72]). Engaging student emotions is, however, not free of risk. Greater awareness and concern can trigger pessimism, and even negative impacts on mental health (Jensen, 2002[73]).

Given sufficient space and support, challenging emotions can be channelled constructively towards a heightened sense of responsibility and motivation to look out for solutions in collaboration with others (Chawla, 2022[38]; Lehtonen, Salonen and Cantell, 2018[74]). Lausselet and Zosso (2022[75]) illustrate how an age-appropriate learning progression in this field could look like. Their framework, reflected in Table 1, displays an evolution from early childhood, emphasising foundational bonds with nature and feelings of safety, to more intricate engagements in later stages.

In primary education, students are encouraged towards guided exploration, strengthening connection with the environment. In secondary school, the focus shifts to independent exploration and deepening commitment to environmental concerns, with students beginning to think about the systemic nature of environmental challenges. By upper secondary education, the curriculum advocates for a more reflexive approach, pushing students to apply their knowledge as they reach out to and act in their communities, communicate about environmental concerns and network with various actors. The outlined bonds, ranging from inclusive to performative, signify the depth and nature of the student-environment relationship at each stage.

Table 1. Age-appropriate outdoor environmental education

Learning progression for outdoor environmental education in early childhood, primary and secondary education

Early childhood (4-8-year-olds)	**Primary** (8-12-year-olds)	**Lower secondary** (12-15-year-olds)	**Upper secondary** (over 15 years old)
Sense of belonging	Exploration (guided)	Exploration (autonomous)	Reflexivity
Feeling safe within the environment	Adaptation (place <-> self)	Adaptation (place <-> self) and commitment	Commitment
Sense of well-being in the environment	Sense of well-being in the environment	Thinking the environment and myself in it	Communication to and with others about environment
Awakening to the complexity and richness of the environment	Caring for the environment	Caring for the environment	Networking with societal actors for the environment
Curiosity (about the living world)	Curiosity (about biodiversity) and understanding	Prospective curiosity (about possible transformations of the environment)	Action and agency
Inclusive bond	**Adaptive bond**	**Transformative bond**	**Performative bond**

Source: Lausselet and Zosso (2022[75]), Bonding with the World: A Pedagogical Approach In: Jucker, R., von Au, J. (eds), High-Quality Outdoor Learning. Springer, Cham. https://doi.org/10.1007/978-3-031-04108-2_15

In addition to matching educational goals and students' developmental stages, an effective curriculum must also be culturally relevant to the students it serves. Research on human learning has recognised that learning in schools "may be facilitated if the out-of-school cultural practices of students are viewed as resources, tools, or assets" (National Academies of Sciences, Engineering, and Medicine, 2018[76]). In grounding instruction in local phenomena, PBE can incorporate students' unique perspectives into the curriculum and show one way in which culturally responsive instruction can be accomplished. All the same, given the diverse experiences that students bring into the classroom, their perceptions of a place and community can vary, which also poses challenges for instructional design.

Some scholars point out that a potential issue arises when the idea of place is subject to restrictive interpretations (McInerney, Smyth and Down, 2011[77]). There is a risk that PBE programmes present places as static and clearly defined, overlooking their dynamic and interconnected nature. Places are multifaceted and shaped by factors such as politics, race, gender, and class, which influence the relation individuals establish with them. Challenges appear when an idealised view of places neglects the challenging realities faced by those in less scenic or socially divided areas. In line with views stressing the civic and political aspects of PBE, the perspectives expressed here highlight the need to critically assess the physical, social, and cultural aspects of places, acknowledging student identities in the process.

Giving students voice in defining the themes and projects they will work on is one way to do this. The point is not for teachers to let students do what they want but negotiating the articulation of the programme with them, making them feel comfortable and motivated while ensuring the learning plan connects to the intended curriculum. Research shows that students in service-learning programmes are often given the opportunity to select the activity that best suits them, and that matching students' preferences in this way can increase the benefits of the intervention (Moely, Furco and Reed, 2008[78]).

Source: (Nusche, Fuster Rabella and Lauterbach, 2024[13]) "Rethinking Education in the Context of Climate Change: Leverage Points for Transformative Change", OECD Education Working Papers, No. 307, OECD Publishing, Paris, https://doi.org/10.1787/f14c8a81-en.

Beyond the school sector, students in higher levels of education will also need opportunities to gain practical experience working with environmental challenges as part of their education (Molderez and Fonseca, 2018[79]). In higher education institutions (HEIs), for example, place-based learning can happen when a higher education campus re-organises itself as a "living lab" and active learning space to promote experiential learning and problem-solving. In the Netherlands, for example, "green offices" exist in almost every HEI. These offices run activities with students and teachers to undertake sustainable projects, or design new sustainability-focused courses, often focused on the immediate campus environment and curriculum (Green Office Movement, n.d.[80]; OECD, 2023[81]).

Service learning is seen as another valuable method to implement PBE (OECD, 2023[82]; Drewery and Lollar, 2024[83]). Service learning can be defined as "a course-based, credit-bearing educational experience in which students (a) participate in an organised service activity that meets identified community needs and (b) reflect on the service activity in such a way as to gain further understanding of course content, a broader appreciation of the discipline, and an enhanced sense of personal values and civic responsibility" (Bringle and Hatcher, 1999, p. 180[84]). While there is no comparable international evidence on the extent to which and how HEIs in different countries engage in service learning, it is common practice in almost all HEIs in the United States (OECD, 2019[85]). In Europe, service learning has been much slower to develop and only started appearing in the 2000s. In 2019, the European Observatory for Service Learning in Higher Education (EOSLHE) found that at least 29 European countries had some level of activity of service learning, although this is not at all systematic (EOSLHE, 2020[86]).

In recent years, service learning has been used by many HEIs to link the curriculum to environmental challenges facing local communities. In many cases, such collaboration has also involved collaboration with the local school community, thereby fostering the development of practice-based research and continuing professional learning around sustainability for the teaching community (OECD, 2023[87]; OECD, 2023[87]). For example, Lancaster university in England (United Kingdom) has adopted a place-based approach centred on finding solutions to protect the environment in the Morecambe Bay to develop its higher education curricula. This is done in close collaboration with higher education and local school students, teachers, researchers and other community actors to "develop a locally-anchored and progressive curriculum which from early years to postgraduate, provide[s] the green skills, knowledge and behaviours required by industry to respond to the climate emergency" (Lancaster University, n.d.[88]) (see also Chapter 2).

Designing education and training policies that foster agency for socio-behavioural change

The identification of key "sustainability competencies" is an important step towards integrating sustainability into education. However, the real challenge lies in translating such learning goals and competency frameworks into actionable strategies within education systems. For effective implementation, these frameworks need to be embedded into education and training curricula, integrated in initial education and continuing professional learning for educators, as well as reflected in assessment and evaluation frameworks (Nusche, Fuster Rabella and Lauterbach, 2024[13]). Without such active support and integration, the frameworks risk remaining theoretical, without bringing the intended transformative impact on learners and educators. Therefore, beyond having these frameworks in place, concerted efforts are required to ensure they are effectively used to drive change within education systems.

Embedding sustainability in curricula, qualifications and study programmes

OECD and European Commission analyses show that the inclusion of sustainability among topics in curricula for compulsory education has become near universal in European and OECD countries (OECD, 2020[89]; OECD, 2022[19]; European Commission, 2024[90]). Yet, curriculum designers, including teachers themselves, face ongoing challenges of deciding which aspects to prioritise and where best to integrate them in often already overloaded curricula. For example, while Earth system science naturally finds its place in natural science curricula, the interactions of Earth systems with human activity and the intricate socio-ecological challenges of climate change fit equally well in social science curricula. OECD (2020[89]) found that countries vary widely with respect to the subjects in which environmental sustainability issues are covered, ranging from science and humanities subjects, to mathematics, technology/home economics, national language, arts and physical education/health.

Going further, due to the inter-disciplinary nature of sustainability challenges and their wide-reaching impacts on all aspects of life, many curricula establish it not just within specific subjects but as a cross-curricular priority. The OECD's Curriculum Content Mapping (CCM), which analysed curriculum goals for primary and secondary education in 37 countries and jurisdictions, found that environmental sustainability was the most frequently cited transversal theme included in countries' overarching goals for education (OECD, 2020[89]).

In upper secondary and post-secondary education and training, where providers are more autonomous in developing curriculum content than in lower levels of schooling, there is potentially more scope for adding specific courses, programmes and qualifications addressing sustainability topics. Adding new content related to sustainability requires choosing between adapting existing courses (which requires finding a link to existing content), creating additional formal courses, or expanding opportunities for applied learning, such as experiential, challenge-based or work-based learning (which may require the omission of other courses) (OECD, 2023[82]; OECD, 2024[91]).

Interdisciplinary approaches are being incentivised in many school systems. Norway's core curriculum, for example, has citizenship and sustainable development as one of three overarching curriculum development topics, alongside health and life skills (Norwegian Education Directorate, 2020[92]). Ireland has sought to embed climate action and sustainability as a cross-curricular topic at all levels of education and has recently introduced the Leaving Certificate Climate Action and Sustainable Development (CASD) specification in the Senior Cycle. A recent consultation process has revealed some of the challenges and opportunities in developing this new sustainability-focused course (Box 2.8).

Box 2.8. Leaving Certificate Climate Action and Sustainable Development in Ireland

Since the introduction of a national strategy on Education for Sustainable Development (ESD) in 2014, Ireland has sought to embed climate action and ESD at all levels of education including in early childhood, primary, and secondary education, fostering vertical and horizontal alignment in the curriculum. Ireland's cross-curricular approach meant that different subjects were expected to cover different, but complementary, elements of ESD. For example, in upper secondary education (Senior Cycle), Agricultural Science addresses the use of natural resources at local, national, and global levels, and the role of the agri-food industry in climate change, among other issues. ESD also promotes links across areas of knowledge, such as reinforcing the interdependence of scientific, economic, and social dimensions within Leaving Certificate Agricultural Science.

Ireland's commitment to climate action and sustainable development has remained steadfast, though its approach to ESD has evolved over the years as articulated in the 2nd National Strategy – ESD to 2030. A key development is the introduction of the Leaving Certificate Climate Action and Sustainable Development (CASD) specification in the Senior Cycle. The subject will initially be introduced in a small number of schools, called Phase One schools, from 2025. The introduction of this new subject is part of a broader Senior Cycle redevelopment programme, announced in 2022.

CASD's overarching aim is to develop students' capacity for informed and meaningful action toward a just and sustainable world. It will provide Senior Cycle students with a foundational knowledge of climate science, while encouraging them to explore their roles as global citizens. The subject will examine systems of decision making, the drivers of global poverty, the root causes of climate and sustainability issues, and environmental injustice. Additionally, CASD will leverage innovative teaching and learning approaches to promote student voice, critical thinking, creativity, and collective and democratic action. The subject aims to foster solidarity with communities affected by climate change, and students will engage with these challenges through an interdisciplinary, solutions-focused approach that prepares them to contribute meaningfully to a sustainable future. An Additional Assessment Component - an Action Project, worth 40% of the total available marks - will offer students opportunities to pursue their interests, make autonomous decisions, acquire conceptual understanding, and self-regulate their learning.

Consultation on the draft CASD specification (NCCA, 2024[93]) was overall very positive regarding its rationale and aims. However, challenges were raised, including potential overlap with other existing subject areas, particularly Geography, and concerns about which teachers would be qualified to teach the course. There was also discussion about maintaining the status of CASD compared to traditional single-discipline subjects. Nonetheless, there are significant opportunities, such as the potential to introduce new curricular structures, with the Action Project broadly welcomed—provided its manageability is addressed. The final specification was published in early September 2024.

Source: (NCCA, 2024[94]) Draft Leaving Certificate Climate Action and Sustainable Development Specification; (NCCA, 2024[95]) Background Paper and Brief for the Development of Leaving Certificate Climate Action and Sustainable Development; (NCCA, 2024[93]) Report on the Consultation on the Draft Specification for Leaving Certificate Climate Action and Sustainable Development; (OECD, 2023[96]) "Implementation of Ireland's Leaving Certificate 2020-2021: Lessons from the COVID-19 Pandemic", OECD Education Policy Perspectives, No. 73, OECD Publishing, Paris, https://doi.org/10.1787/e36a10b8-en.

Although most countries establish overarching cross-curricular goals for education and training, implementation of these interdisciplinary goals in teaching practice is often challenging, due to the traditional organisation of schools and other educational institutions where learning is often organised around strict subject and disciplinary boundaries and teaching is organised as an individual rather than a collaborative practice (OECD, 2013[97]; OECD, 2019[98]). Curriculum realisation challenges are often compounded by the existence of narrow evaluation and assessment systems that lag behind countries' broader, competency-based learning objectives (Nusche, Fuster Rabella and Lauterbach, 2024[13]). By contrast, an emphasis on assessment *for* and *as* learning may help promote more innovative formats of assessment (OECD, 2013[97]), and there are also various ways to rethink standardised assessments to include complex skills like problem-solving, creativity and communication (Foster and Piacentini, 2023[68]).

In higher education as well, many countries are seeking to develop greater interdisciplinarity, for example by incentivising higher education institutions (HEIs) to develop programmes which integrate knowledge from various fields such as science, economics and social and political studies (Carme Gual, 2019[99]). This is based on the premise that complex global challenges are multidimensional in nature and cannot be understood or resolved from individual disciplinary perspectives (Jacob, 2015[100]). But here, also, this often conflicts with traditional academic staff organisation and reward structures that tend to prioritise research output and publications in high-impact journals, which are typically discipline-specific. To support curriculum adaptation processes, governments can foster collaboration across key stakeholders to map the extent to which sustainability is covered in curricula at various levels of education, identify gap areas and develop guidance and frameworks to support curriculum adaptation (see Box 2.9 for an example from Denmark).

Box 2.9. Mapping curriculum coverage of sustainability content in Denmark

In January 2022, the Danish government adopted an Action Plan on Education for Sustainable Development (ESD). This was developed in response to a review carried out by the Nordic Council of Ministers which found that sustainability is described more implicitly in Danish curricula than in Finland, Iceland, Norway and Sweden (Secretary of the Nordic Council of Ministers and Nordic Council of Ministers, 2021[101]). This led to the establishment of a national partnership, involving representatives from all levels of education, including VET and higher education, to review the state of play of ESD in all levels of education and training. The national review informed the publication of a report in September 2022 including concrete recommendations on how to strengthen ESD in the national learning and assessment practices in all levels of education and training (UBU, 2022[102]).

Source: (Secretary of the Nordic Council of Ministers and Nordic Council of Ministers, 2021[101]) *Mapping Education for Sustainability in the Nordic Countries*, Nordic Co-Operation, https://www.norden.org/en/publication/mapping-education-sustainability-nordic-countries (accessed on 9 March 2023); (UBU, 2022[102]) *PÅ VEJ MOD UDDANNELSER FOR BÆREDYGTIG UDVIKLING*, Government of Denmark, https://verdensmaalene.cdn.prismic.io/verdensmaalene/0f0df43a-2e4a-463e-bc4d-5af1330bf793_UBU_rapport_sept22.pdf (accessed on 9 March 2023).

Bringing place-based approaches to scale

As discussed above, place-based, collaborative, project-based and experiential approaches can be powerful ways to empower learners to exercise agency. They can also address equity concerns by responding to diverse local needs and perspectives and facilitating various forms of expression, thereby engaging a broader range of student profiles and families in the local community.

A key challenge for these approaches, however, is to move beyond isolated "islands of good practice" within individual classrooms or courses and bring effective approaches to scale. Schools and educational providers, positioned between the practice of individual teachers and the broad directives of system-wide policy, have a key role to play in supporting such practices. Educational institutions can offer a clear vision and related structures for embedding sustainable learning and action throughout all aspects of institutional life.

This idea is encapsulated by the term "whole-school" or "whole-institution approach" to sustainability. By integrating sustainability into the institution's operations and infrastructure, and linking these actions to student learning, a more holistic educational experience is cultivated. Because educational institutions are large consumers of goods and services, "greening" their operations, such as in reducing their energy consumption, is a positive step in and of itself (OECD, 2021[103]). Going further, making students an active part of this process provides them with authentic learning experiences to apply their knowledge (Okada and Gray, 2023[104]).

A more widespread adoption of whole-institution approaches within education and training systems requires synergies between the leadership at the institution and community levels and the strategic policy frameworks enacted by governments. Additionally, system-level policies are essential in providing the frameworks, resources, and incentives for educational providers to prioritise place-based action. For example, granting recognition to providers that incorporate sustainability considerations in all aspects of their operations, such as in "green" labelling programmes like Eco-schools (Foundation for Environmental Education, n.d.[105]), can be an effective form of external pressure to raise students' environmental literacy (Boeve-de Pauw and Van Petegem, 2017[106]; Byrne et al., 2023[107]; Cincera and Krajhanzl, 2013[108]). Policies to build capacity can include self-evaluation guidelines for schools to systematically review their initiatives and measure progress.

Adapting initial education and continuing professional learning for educators

Although most countries establish overarching cross-curricular goals for education and training, implementation of these interdisciplinary goals in teaching practice is often challenging, if not adequately supported. This is due to the traditional organisation of schools and other educational institutions where learning is often organised around strict subject and disciplinary boundaries and teaching is organised as an individual rather than a collaborative practice (OECD, 2013[97]; OECD, 2019[98]). Additionally, subject teachers often find it challenging to link climate change content to their discipline, adding further difficulties. Little internationally comparable information is available on teachers' engagement with topics, but comprehensive information will become available from the OECD's 2024 Teaching and Learning International Survey (TALIS).

Box 2.10. Forthcoming OECD data on teachers' engagement with sustainability

The OECD's Teaching and Learning International Survey (TALIS) 2024 will collect a rich set of internationally comparable indicators on teachers' engagement with environmental and sustainability education and climate change education. This will offer information on different aspects of teachers' engagement with these topics, including their attitudes towards sustainability and climate education, their attitudes towards climate change itself (such as their level of concern), their professional opportunities to learn about climate change, and the barriers they experience to teaching about climate change. TALIS also includes a principal questionnaire and collects information on actions taken by principals to adapting school infrastructure in the context of climate change. Once collected, the data will allow policymakers to evaluate different characteristics of teachers and teaching related to climate change and sustainability. The initial report from TALIS 2024 will be released in October 2025 and a dedicated report on teachers' engagement with environmental, sustainability and climate change education will follow in 2026.

Source: (Nusche, Fuster Rabella and Lauterbach, 2024[13]) "Rethinking education in the context of climate change: Leverage points for transformative change", OECD Education Working Papers, No. 307, OECD Publishing, Paris, https://doi.org/10.1787/f14c8a81-en.

In most countries, initial teacher education (ITE) is delivered by teacher education institutes operating in highly autonomous HEIs, making the integration of sustainability across ITE curricula delivered by different HEIs challenging (OECD, 2022[19]). Evidence also shows that ITE curricula primarily address sustainability issues as an elective course or on a project basis (Tasiopoulou et al, 2022[109]; Evans, 2019[110]). In addition, sustainability topics are mainly addressed in those ITE curricula that prepare teachers specifically for the subjects that have the closest link to climate change, such as Geography or Science, but not systematically in all ITE courses, which is at odds with the cross-curricular nature of the objective in many countries.

In Europe, the European Commission carried out a comprehensive assessment of the inclusion of sustainability in regulations or guidelines for ITE and found that less than half of the education systems studied have regulations or guidelines that include sustainability education in ITE. While these provisions often apply to all prospective teachers, they are sometimes specific to certain subjects. About a third of systems address the understanding of sustainability issues, while a dozen systems focus on interdisciplinary teaching that promotes critical thinking, problem-solving, and respect for diverse values. Fewer systems address partnerships connecting learners with nature and global communities. The implementation of these guidelines can vary significantly, as ITE providers typically enjoy autonomy in developing their programmes. In some cases, sustainability-related content is incorporated even without explicit regulations, especially when sustainability is part of the national curriculum. The existence of these regulations signals efforts by public authorities to integrate sustainability in education, though variation in operationalisation and evaluation can lead to uneven implementation across regions (European Commission, 2024[90])

In Ireland, to strengthen consistency in how different providers approach ITE, all HEIs offering ITE must obtain accreditation from the Teaching Council and meet seven standards. One of these is "Global Citizenship Education" and includes a focus on education for sustainable development (The Teaching Council, 2020[111]). In Finland, alignment of ITE curricula is supported through the Teacher Education Forum, which was established in 2016 by the Ministry of Education. The Forum provides a platform for teacher educators, VET and schoolteachers, municipalities, researchers, students and other relevant stakeholders to engage in research-based collaboration through literature reviews, peer learning and benchmarking. These activities centre on national guidelines and priorities for the further development of teacher education in Finland, one of which is climate change (Ministry of Education and Culture, 2022[112]). In the French Community of Belgium (FWB), a recent reform of initial teacher education has also included a focus on developing teacher educators' environmental sustainability literacy (see Box 2.11).

Box 2.11. Integration of education for sustainability in initial teacher education in the French Community of Belgium

In 2019, the French Community of Belgium started a major reform of its initial teacher education system. One of the main objectives of the reform was to support teacher educators to develop pedagogies in support of social and intercultural competencies among learners, notably to enable them to act as responsible citizens for their school and local community.

To support the implementation of this specific action in relation to environmental sustainability, a Commission on Sustainable Development from the Academy of Research and Higher Education developed a set of guidelines on how HEIs ca implement ESD into teacher training curricula. The report recommends three major approaches:

1) The integration of transversal competencies related to ESD across all disciplines (e.g. an introductory module on ESD and the socio-ecological transition as a common course for all teacher educators);
2) The development of specific competencies on ESD, linked to the specific discipline(s) or course(s) for which teachers educators are being prepared (i.e. integration in existing ITE courses); and
3) Inclusion of opportunities for experiential learning and experimentation related to environmental sustainability in all ITE curricula.

Source: Based on FWB (2019[113]), *Décret définissant la formation initiale des enseignants [Decree on initial teacher education]*, French Community of Belgium (FWB), https://www.gallilex.cfwb.be/fr/leg_res_02.php?ncda=46261&referant=l01 (accessed on 2 September 2024).and (2022[114]), *Mise en oeuvre du décret relatif à la formation initiale des enseignants au développement durable [Implementation of the decree on initial teacher education for sustainable development]*, Academy of Research and Higher Education (ARES), https://rfie.ares-ac.be/ressources/th%C3%A9matiques-transversales/d%C3%A9veloppement-durable (accessed on 2 September 2024).

The integration of sustainability topics in continuing professional learning also needs strengthening (this is discussed in more detail in the section on Building a coherent skills delivery landscape for the green transition). Interdisciplinary approaches are becoming more common across professions as a way of responding to contemporary and future challenges (McGrath, 2023[115]; Helvaci and Helvaci, 2019[116]), making it necessary for all professions, including teachers, to engage in continuing professional learning to acquire relevant skills of working this way (Lawson and Veen, 2016[117]). For teachers, potential opportunities for professional learning include working with other teachers as well as partnerships with other professionals (McGrath, 2023[115]; Day, 2002[118]). This can lead to career specialisation focuses related to curriculum interests (Song and Wang, 2021[119]; Wang et al., 2020[120]; Choi et al., 2022[121]). To be successful, schools will need to be supported to develop positive and sustainable professional networks that add to the value of schooling in a meaningful way (OECD, 2024[122]).

For HEIs, which might play a key role in developing the cross-disciplinary integration of sustainability considerations, specifically recognising and encouraging efforts of staff to collaborate across faculties and departments and break down disciplinary barriers can be crucial in motivating these professional learning efforts (Ashby and Exter, 2018[123]; OECD, 2024[91]). Incentives for interdisciplinary collaboration within higher education can be developed at institution and system level. National teaching awards, for example, recognising outstanding individuals or teams, are present in around half of European higher education systems (Bunescu and Gaebel, 2018[124]).

In Germany, the Research and Transfer Centre "Sustainability and Climate Impact Management" (FTZ-NK) at the Hamburg University of Applied Sciences is an example of how academic staff from various disciplines within a single institution can be incentivised to join forces to address global challenges (Molthan-Hill et al., 2019[125]; HAW Hamburg, 2024[126]). The Centre's International Climate Change Information and Research Programme (ICCIRP) encourages research from doctoral students in critical areas of sustainability and climate change. It also facilitates education and communication about climate change through workshops and conferences, thereby facilitating inter-disciplinary collaboration across the institution around climate change. Similarly, teacher educators from Tallinn University in Estonia reported that the integration of sustainability in their curricula worked as a powerful incentive for teacher educators to collaborate with climate change experts from other faculties (OECD, 2023[87]).

Promoting engagement in sustainability learning beyond formal education

Formal, informal and non-formal learning all play a critical role in fostering agency among learners of all ages and motivating actions tackling the climate and other environmental crises. Individuals learn constantly, being able to accumulate knowledge, skills and competences throughout their lifetimes, often extending well beyond the boundaries of organised formal education.

Learning may occur at the initiative of the individual but also happens as a by-product of more organised activities, whether or not the activities themselves have learning objectives (Werquin, 2010[127]). Evidence indicates however that non-formal education programs can have long-term impacts, with studies showing lasting educational, economic, and mental health benefits, especially when programs build life skills, foster community connections, and emphasise gender equality (Simac, Marcus and Harper, 2019[128]). This section explores avenues for extending information and learning opportunities beyond the formal education sector.

Information campaigns and consumer education

Studies have shown that well-executed communication strategies and targeted campaigns, have the potential to contribute to enhancing understanding and engagement, leading to more informed and active participation in environmental initiatives (Ockwell, Whitmarsh and O'Neill, 2009[129]; Segerberg, 2017[130]; Goldberg et al., 2021[131]; Gulliver, Fielding and Louis, 2019[132]; Green et al., 2019[133]).

Public communication and awareness-raising campaigns often offer effective learning opportunities that significantly influence public perception and action regarding climate change, shaping agendas at local, national, and international levels (Khatibi et al., 2021[10]). With increasing internet access, online and social media platforms have become crucial for engaging the public, informing them about climate issues, and mobilizing action (Segerberg, 2017[130]). Campaigns are typically articulated around four main goals: (i) to inform, raise awareness, and shape public understanding about the science, problems, and politics of climate change; (ii) to change consumer and citizen behaviour; (iii) to network and connect concerned publics; and (iv) to visibly mobilise consumers or citizens to put pressure on decision-makers (Segerberg, 2017[130]).

Consumer education initiatives can play a potentially important role in fostering informed and sustainable behaviours. Barriers to sustainable consumption are multifaceted, ranging from a lack of viable alternatives and reliable information to psychological factors like low motivation and trust issues (Capgemini, 2021[134]; European Commission: Directorate-General for Environment, 2020[135]). To address these challenges, several remedies have been identified that aim to target the intention-action gap by making sustainable choices more accessible and appealing to consumers. These include interventions such as information provision, green claims, that is, a statement made by a company or product suggesting that it is environmentally friendly or sustainable, and eco- labels to improve the visibility of sustainable options.

For example, Schubert (2017[136]) shows that highlighting the importance of sustainable product features or simplifying related information can leverage consumer interest in adopting greener choices. In addition, by leveraging social norms to promote conformity and pro-environmental behaviour, consumers' actions can be influenced as they tend to base their behaviour on the observed or inferred actions of others. (Schultz, Khazian and Zaleski, 2008[137]; Kormos, Gifford and Brown, 2014[138]). Lastly, green defaults, which make sustainable choices the path of least resistance, can effectively leverage consumers' tendency to stick with the status quo and promote pro-environmental behaviour. For example, Liebe, Gewinner and Diekmann (2021[139]) found that when renewable energy was presented as the default option to existing customers, approximately 80% of both household and business clients chose to remain with the green energy alternative and that that effect was largely stable over time.

Education plays a critical role in shaping these attitudes and behaviours, as higher levels of education are often associated with greater environmental awareness and a stronger willingness to act, as discussed, and to adopt sustainable practices in particular (Piao and Managi, 2023[140]). Over recent years, there has been a steady rise in the number of studies focusing on education and sustainable consumption, as schools, universities, along with information campaigns play a crucial role in shaping the ideas and attitudes of populations (de Oliveira et al., 2022[141]). Education plays a role in disseminating information about the benefits, either global or personal, of adopting sustainable practices. Fischer and Barth (2014[142]) argue that transversal competencies are essential for addressing the complex challenges of sustainable consumption, advocating for a broad and effective educational strategy that goes beyond merely training skills, providing information, and testing for results. Al-Nuaimi and Al-Ghamdi (2022[143]) show that higher education institutions play a key role in promoting sustainable consumption through both formal curricula and experiential learning opportunities, which help students internalize sustainable practices and contribute to broader environmental initiatives on campus.

Science-based activism

The increased collaboration of activists with scientists and researchers represents new learning opportunities for all those involved, outside of formal education settings. Many scholars are now focusing on research that supports activism, though traditional research impact metrics still often undervalue this contribution (McLaren et al., 2024[144]). For example, through a series of online workshops, both activists and academics from several European countries came together to share experiences and to develop proposals for future research that can support activism (McLaren et al., 2024[144]). This partnership can yield results in the near and mid-term in influencing public awareness and policy.

Accompanying this surge in climate activism and campaigning, the advances in attribution science (Stuart-Smith et al., 2021[145]) and fruitful collaboration between activists, scientist and lawyers have led to a steep increase in climate litigation worldwide (Figure 2.13), where individuals, communities, and environmental groups seek accountability and justice through the courts. By improving the ability to link specific environmental events and trends directly to human activities, particularly GHG emissions (Stuart-Smith et al., 2021[145]; Pfrommer et al., 2019[146]), this scientific progress has provided stronger evidence for legal claims. Again here, there are learning opportunities for all stakeholders involved that go beyond formal education.

Figure 2.13. Increase in number of climate litigation cases

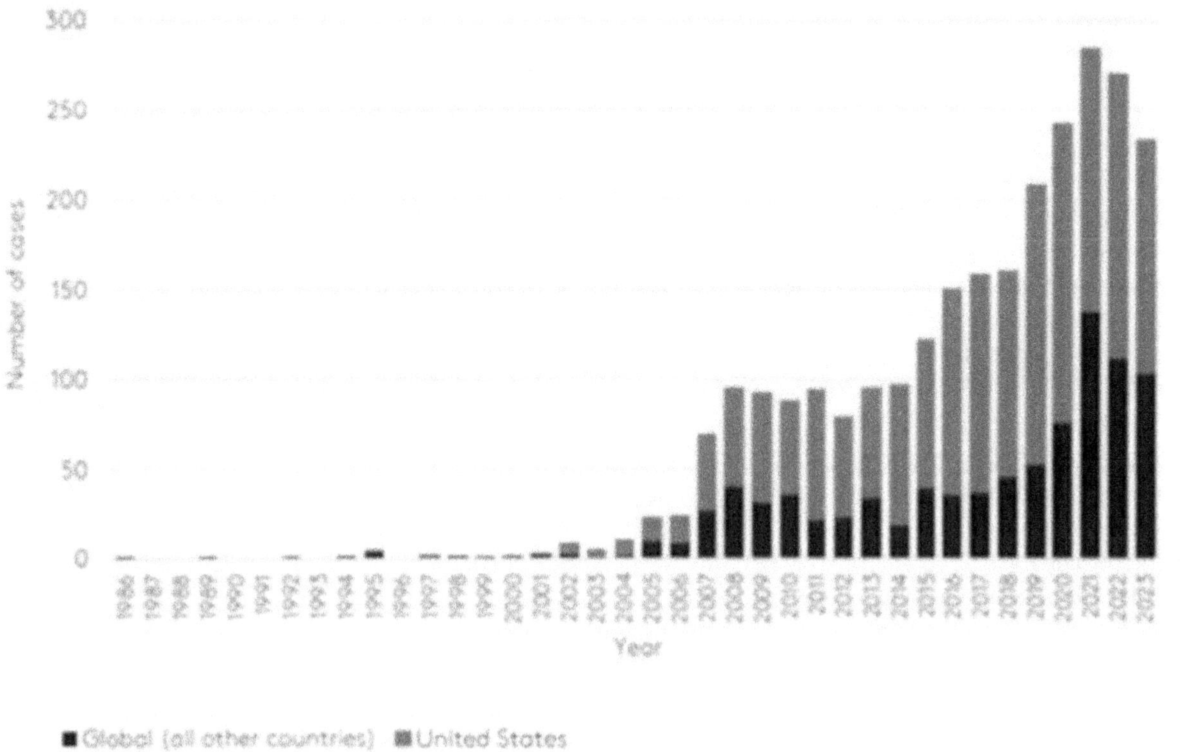

Source: (Setzer J and Higham C, 2024[147]) Global Trends in Climate Change Litigation: 2024 Snapshot, Grantham Research Institute on Climate Change and the Environment, London School of Economics and Political Science, https://www.lse.ac.uk/granthaminstitute/wp-content/uploads/2024/06/Global-trends-in-climate-change-litigation-2024-snapshot.pdf (accessed on 3 October 2024).

Towards a strategic approach to science communication

Higher education can play a key role in helping individuals across all layers of society develop an understanding of the systemic nature of climate change, and their role in it. To achieve this, however, higher education itself will need to adapt the way in which it delivers education and engages with wider society.

In a world where social media and digital platforms have radically altered the science communication landscape, mis- and disinformation have become large-scale and widespread, including climate change related disinformation and climate change denial (OECD, 2023[148]). As beacons of science and innovation, HEIs have an ethical duty to not only produce evidence-based information about the causes, consequences and possible solutions to climate change, but also to engage with society to communicate this information in a transparent and reliable way.

For many academics, however, science communication is carried out on an ad hoc or one-off project basis rather than being a core part of their (research) activities. A survey of more than 7 000 full-time academics at HEIs in 13 countries[7] across the world has found that full-time academics tend to spend only 7% of their time on service and engagement on average. 30% of their annualised hours are spent on teaching, around 40% on research activities, and about 15% on administration (Bentley and Kyvik, 2012[149]). A lack of time, (financial) resources, training and recognition for engaging in effective science communication are cited as some of the main reasons for the lack of more continual engagement in science communication by academic staff (OECD, 2023[150]).

There are indications, however, that science communication has become more important in recent years for many HEIs. A survey by the International Association of Universities covering 111 jurisdictions has found that 45% of respondents said that they engaged and increased their public outreach activity during the COVID-19 pandemic (Marinoni, Van't Land and Jensen, 2020[151]). Climate change, another global challenge, may be used as an equally powerful lever to mobilise the higher education sector to engage ore actively in science communication.

To develop science communication in higher education, governments can support the development of institutional and national support structures for academic staff. In an effort to bundle resources and facilitate collaboration, some HEIs have set up a dedicated unit to support academic staff with science communication. For example, Durham University in England (United Kingdom) has a dedicated Science and Communication Outreach Department which supports academic staff to engage and establish partnerships with local and global actors, businesses, government and civil society (Durham University, n.d.[152]). At system level, public authorities in the United Kingdom and the Netherlands have funded the development of guidelines for HEIs on how to support and reward scientists who work structurally on science communication (RCUK, 2020[153]; KNAW, 2022[154]). Some countries have also set up national support centres for science communication to promote peer learning among academics engaged in science communication. Examples are Germany's Science in Dialogue Centre (*Wissenschaft im Dialog*) (Wissenschaft im Dialog, n.d.[155]), the National Centre for Science Communication in the Netherlands (Dutch Ministry of Education, Culture and Science, 2022[156]), or the National Co-Ordinating Centre for Public Engagement in the United Kingdom (NCCPE, n.d.[157]).

In conclusion, scaling climate solutions requires a multifaceted approach where informal and non-formal learning can play a crucial role in fostering agency and willingness to adopt sustainable behaviours. Informal and non-formal learning avenues complement formal education by providing focused, practical, hands-on experiences and continuous learning opportunities that empower individuals to act on climate issues. By integrating these diverse educational approaches, policymakers can create a robust framework that drives meaningful action tackling climate and other environmental challenges.

References

Al-Menshawi, A. and S. Abu Al-Yazeed (2020), "Developing Skills of Systemic Thinking for Secondary Students", *International Journal of Instructional Technology and Educational Studies*, Vol. 1/1, pp. 31-33, https://doi.org/10.21608/ihites.2020.29074.1014. [62]

Al-Nuaimi, S. and S. Al-Ghamdi (2022), "Sustainable Consumption and Education for Sustainability in Higher Education", *Sustainability*, Vol. 14/12, p. 7255, https://doi.org/10.3390/su14127255. [143]

Aoyagi, M. et al. (2024), *World Newspaper Coverage of Climate Change or Global Warming, 2004-2024.*, https://sciencepolicy.colorado.edu/icecaps/research/media_coverage/world/index.html (accessed on 5 December 2024). [40]

ARES (2022), *Mise en oeuvre du décret relatif à la formation initial des enseignants [et développement durable [Implementation of the decree on initial teacher education for sustainable development]*, Academy of Research and Higher Education (ARES), https://rfie.ares-ac.be/ressources/th%C3%A9matiques-transversales/d%C3%A9veloppement-durable (accessed on 2 September 2024). [114]

Arias, P. et al. (eds.) (2023), *Climate Change 2023: Synthesis Report. Contribution of Working Groups I, II and III to the Sixth Assessment Report of the Intergovernmental Panel on Climate Change [Core Writing Team, H. Lee and J. Romero (eds.)]. IPCC, Geneva, Switzerland.*, IPCC, Geneva, Switzerland, https://doi.org/10.59327/IPCC/AR6-9789291691647. [3]

Asai, K., F. Borgonovi and S. Wildi (2022), "Understanding how economic conditions and natural disasters shape environmental attitudes: A cross-country comparison to inform policy making", *OECD Social, Employment and Migration Working Papers*, No. 280, OECD Publishing, Paris, https://doi.org/10.1787/8e880ea2-en. [35]

Ashby, A. and M. Exter (2018), "Designing for Interdisciplinarity in Higher Education: Considerations for Instructional Designers", *TechTrends*, Vol. 63, https://link.springer.com/article/10.1007/s11528-018-0352-z. [123]

Assaraf, O. and N. Orion (2009), "System thinking skills at the elementary school level", *Journal of Research in Science Teaching*, Vol. 47/5, pp. 540-563, https://doi.org/10.1002/tea.20351. [61]

Bax, W. et al. (2023), "What Works Best in the School-to-Work Transition?", *OECD: The Network Forum*. [164]

Bentley, P. and S. Kyvik (2012), "Academic work from a comparative perspective: A survey of faculty working time across 13 countries", *Higher Education*, Vol. 63/4, pp. 529-47, https://doi.org/10.1007/S10734-011-9457-4/TABLES/7 (accessed on 28 July 2023). [149]

Ben-Zvi-Assaraf, O. and N. Orion (2010), "Four case studies, six years later: Developing system thinking skills in junior high school and sustaining them over time", *Journal of Research in Science Teaching*, Vol. 47/10, pp. 1253-1280, https://doi.org/10.1002/tea.20383. [54]

Bianchi, G., U. Pisiotis and M. Cabrera Giraldez (2022), *GreenComp - The European Sustainability Competence Framework*, Publications Office of the European Union, Luxembourg. [51]

Bielik, T. et al. (2023), "Characterising the Literature on the Teaching and Learning of System Thinking and Complexity in STEM Education: a Bibliometric Analysis and Research Synthesis", *Journal for STEM Education Research*, Vol. 6/2, pp. 199-231, https://doi.org/10.1007/s41979-023-00087-9. [60]

Boeve-de Pauw, J. and P. Van Petegem (2017), "Eco-school evaluation beyond labels: the impact of environmental policy, didactics and nature at school on student outcomes", *Environmental Education Research*, Vol. 24/9, pp. 1250-1267, https://doi.org/10.1080/13504622.2017.1307327. [106]

Borgonovi, F. et al. (2022), "The environmental sustainability competence toolbox: From leaving a better planet for our children to leaving better children for our planet", *OECD Social, Employment and Migration Working Papers*, No. 275, OECD Publishing, Paris, https://doi.org/10.1787/27991ec0-en. [166]

Brannen, S., C. Haig and K. Schmidt (2020), *The age of mass protests - understanding an escalating global trend*, CSIS, https://csis-website-prod.s3.amazonaws.com/s3fs-public/publication/200303_MassProtests_V2.pdf (accessed on 4 September 2024). [41]

Brehm, J. and H. Gruhl (2024), "Increase in concerns about climate change following climate strikes and civil disobedience in Germany", *Nature Communications*, Vol. 15/1, https://doi.org/10.1038/s41467-024-46477-4. [43]

Bringle, R. and J. Hatcher (1999), "Reflection in Service Learning: Making Meaning or Experience", *Evaluation/Reflection*, Vol. 23, pp. 179-185, https://digitalcommons.unomaha.edu/slceeval/23/ (accessed on 4 April 2023). [84]

Bunescu, L. and M. Gaebel (2018), "National Initiatives in Learning and Teaching in Europe", *A report from the European Forum for Enhanced Collaboration in Teaching (EFFECT) project. Brussels: European University Association*, https://eua.eu/downloads/publications/national%20initiatives%20in%20learning%20and%20teaching%20in%20europe.pdf (accessed on 7 November 2023). [124]

Byrne, M. et al. (2023), *Review of the Eco-Schools Environmental Education Programme in Wales (2018-2022)*, Welsh Government, Cardiff, https://www.gov.wales/eco-schools-programme-wales-review-april-2018-january-2022 (accessed on 11 December 2023). [107]

Capgemini (2021), *Consumer Products and Retail - How sustainability is fundamentally changing consumer preferences*, https://www.capgemini.com/wp-content/uploads/2021/02/20-06_9880_Sustainability-in-CPR_Final_Web-1-2.pdf (accessed on 2 September 2024). [134]

Carme Gual (2019), "Are universities ready to have a real impact on achieving the sustainable development goals (SDGs)?", in Josep M. Vilalta et al. (eds.), *Implementing the 2030 Agenda at Higher Education Institutions: Challenges and Responses*. [99]

Carnegie (n.d.), *Carnegie Endowment for International Peace's Climate Protest Tracker*, https://carnegieendowment.org/features/climate-protest-tracker?lang=en (accessed on 5 December 2024). [46]

Chancel, L. et al. (2022), *World Inequality Report 2022*, World Inequality Lab, https://wir2022.wid.world/ (accessed on 9 December 2024). [50]

Chawla, L. (2022), "Childhood Nature Connection and Constructive Hope: Helping Young People Connect with Nature and Cope with Environmental Loss", in Jucker, R. and J. von Au (eds.), *High-Quality Outdoor Learning*. [38]

Choi, S. et al. (2022), "Professional Learning Communities: Supporting Interdisciplinary Teaching in STEM", in *7th STEM in Education Conference 2022 Proceedings*. [121]

Cincera, J. and J. Krajhanzl (2013), "Eco-Schools: what factors influence pupils' action competence for pro-environmental behaviour?", *Journal of Cleaner Production*, Vol. 61, pp. 117-121, https://doi.org/10.1016/j.jclepro.2013.06.030. [108]

Committee on How People Learn II: The Science and Practice of Learning et al. (2018), *How People Learn II*, National Academies Press, Washington, D.C., https://doi.org/10.17226/24783. [162]

Creutzig, F. et al. (2021), "Demand-side solutions to climate change mitigation consistent with high levels of well-being", *Nature Climate Change*, Vol. 12/1, pp. 36-46, https://doi.org/10.1038/s41558-021-01219-y. [6]

Damerell, P., C. Howe and E. Milner-Gulland (2013), "Child-orientated environmental education influences adult knowledge and household behaviour", *Environmental Research Letters*, Vol. 8/1, https://doi.org/10.1088/1748-9326/8/1/015016. [20]

Day, C. (2002), *Developing teachers: The challenges of lifelong learning*, Routledge. [118]

de Oliveira, U. et al. (2022), "Systematic Literature Review on Sustainable Consumption from the Perspective of Companies, People and Public Policies", *Sustainability*, Vol. 14/21, p. 13771, https://doi.org/10.3390/su142113771. [141]

Dhakal, S. et al. (2022), "Emissions Trends and Drivers", in *IPCC, 2022: Climate Change 2022 - Mitigation of Climate Change*, Cambridge University Press, https://doi.org/10.1017/9781009157926.004. [2]

Drewery, M. and J. Lollar (2024), "Undergraduates' perceptions of the value of service-learning", *Frontiers in Education*, Vol. 9, https://doi.org/10.3389/feduc.2024.1330456. [83]

Durham University (n.d.), *Science Outreach and Engagement*, https://www.dur.ac.uk/science.outreach/ (accessed on 14 April 2023). [152]

Dutch Ministry of Education, Culture and Science (2022), *Nederland krijgt nationaal centrum voor wetenschapscommunicatie [Netherlands Gets National Centre for Science Communication]*, Dutch Ministry of Education, Culture and Science, https://www.rijksoverheid.nl/actueel/nieuws/2022/05/25/nederland-krijgt-nationaal-centrum-voor-wetenschapscommunicatie (accessed on 22 June 2023). [156]

Earth4All (2024), *The Earth for All 2024 Survey: Exploring global attitudes to political and economic transformation*, https://earth4all.life/global-survey-2024/. [33]

Elfer, C. (2011), *Place-based education: A review of historical precedents in theory & practice*, https://getd.libs.uga.edu/pdfs/elfer_charles_j_201108_phd.pdf (accessed on 10 October 2023). [67]

EOSLHE (2020), *State of the Art of Service-Learning in European Higher Education*, European Observatory of Service Learning in Higher Education (EOSLHE), https://www.eoslhe.eu/state-of-the-art-of-service-learning-in-european-higher-education/ (accessed on 25 June 2023). [86]

ESS (2016), *ESS round 8 - 2016. Welfare attitudes, Attitudes to climate change*, https://ess.sikt.no/en/study/f8e11f55-0c14-4ab3-abde-96d3f14d3c76 (accessed on 28 August 2024). [30]

European Commission (2024), "Learning for sustainability in Europe: Building competences and supporting teachers and schools", https://doi.org/10.2797/87405. [90]

European Commission: Directorate-General for Environment (2020), *Attitudes of Europeans towards the environment – Report*, European Commission, https://data.europa.eu/doi/10.2779/902489. [135]

European Commission: European Education and Culture Executive Agency (2024), *Learning for sustainability in Europe – Building competences and supporting teachers and schools – Eurydice report*, Publications Office of the European Union, https://data.europa.eu/doi/10.2797/81397. [165]

Evans, T. (2019), "Competencies and Pedagogies for Sustainability Education: A Roadmap for Sustainability Studies Program Development in Colleges and Universities", *Sustainability*, Vol. 11/19, p. 5526, https://doi.org/10.3390/su11195526. [110]

Fischer, D. and M. Barth (2014), "Key Competencies <i>for</i> and <i>beyond</i> Sustainable Consumption An Educational Contribution to the Debate", *GAIA - Ecological Perspectives for Science and Society*, Vol. 23/3, pp. 193-200, https://doi.org/10.14512/gaia.23.s1.7. [142]

Foster, N. and M. Piacentini (eds.) (2023), *Innovating Assessments to Measure and Support Complex Skills*, OECD Publishing, Paris, https://doi.org/10.1787/e5f3e341-en. [68]

Foundation for Environmental Education (n.d.), *About Eco-Schools*, Foundation for Environmental Education, https://www.ecoschools.global/. [105]

Fritz, L. et al. (2023), "Perceived impacts of the Fridays for Future climate movement on environmental concern and behaviour in Switzerland", *Sustainability Science*, Vol. 18/5, pp. 2219-2244, https://doi.org/10.1007/s11625-023-01348-7. [45]

FWB (2019), *Décret définissant la formation initiale des enseignants [Decree on initial teacher education]*, French Community of Belgium (FWB), Brussels, https://www.gallilex.cfwb.be/fr/leg_res_02.php?ncda=46261&referant=l01 (accessed on 2 September 2024). [113]

Gibbs, J. and F. Cappuccio (2022), "Plant-Based Dietary Patterns for Human and Planetary Health", *Nutrients*, Vol. 14/8, p. 1614, https://doi.org/10.3390/nu14081614. [8]

Goldberg, M. et al. (2021), "Shifting Republican views on climate change through targeted advertising", *Nature Climate Change*, Vol. 11/7, pp. 573-577, https://doi.org/10.1038/s41558-021-01070-1. [131]

Green Office Movement (n.d.), *Take the online course to start your Green Office*, https://www.greenofficemovement.org/ (accessed on 7 August 2024). [80]

Green, K. et al. (2019), "A Meta-Analysis of Social Marketing Campaigns to Improve Global Conservation Outcomes", *Social Marketing Quarterly*, Vol. 25/1, pp. 69-87, https://doi.org/10.1177/1524500418824258. [133]

Gulliver, R., K. Fielding and W. Louis (2019), "Understanding the Outcomes of Climate Change Campaigns in the Australian Environmental Movement", *Case Studies in the Environment*, Vol. 3/1, pp. 1-9, https://doi.org/10.1525/cse.2018.001651. [132]

Haasnoot, M. et al. (2013), "Dynamic adaptive policy pathways: A method for crafting robust decisions for a deeply uncertain world", *Global Environmental Change*, Vol. 23/2, pp. 485-498, https://doi.org/10.1016/j.gloenvcha.2012.12.006. [59]

Han, H. and S. Ahn (2020), "Youth Mobilization to Stop Global Climate Change: Narratives and Impact", *Sustainability*, Vol. 12/10, p. 4127, https://doi.org/10.3390/su12104127. [16]

Hargreaves, L. (2008), "The whole-school approach to eduation for sustainable development: From pilot projects to systemic change", *Education for Sustainable Development*, https://www.developmenteducationreview.com/issue/issue-6/whole-school-approach-eduation-sustainable-development-pilot-projects-systemic-change (accessed on 4 April 2023). [69]

HAW Hamburg (2024), *SUSTAINABLE DEVELOPMENT AND CLIMATE CHANGE MANAGEMENT*, https://www.haw-hamburg.de/en/ftz-nk/. [126]

Helvaci, S. and I. Helvaci (2019), "An interdisciplinary environmental education approach: Determining the effects of E-STEM activity on environmental awareness.", *Universal Journal of Educational Research*, Vol. 7/2, pp. 337-346. [116]

Hernandez Gonzalez, F. (2023), "Exploring the Affordances of Place-Based Education for Advancing Sustainability Education: The Role of Cognitive, Socio-Emotional and Behavioural Learning", *Education Sciences*, Vol. 13/7, p. 676, https://doi.org/10.3390/educsci13070676. [71]

Hynes, W., M. Lees and J. Müller (eds.) (2020), *Systemic Thinking for Policy Making: The Potential of Systems Analysis for Addressing Global Policy Challenges in the 21st Century*, New Approaches to Economic Challenges, OECD Publishing, Paris, https://doi.org/10.1787/879c4f7a-en. [57]

IPCC (2022), "Summary for Policymakers", in P.R. Shukla et al. (eds.), *Climate Change 2022: Mitigation of Climate Change. Contribution of Working Group III to the Sixth Assessment Report of the Intergovernmental Panel on Climate Change*, Cambridge University Press, Cambridge, United Kingdom and New York, NY, USA. [1]

IPCC (2018), "Summary for Policymakers", in Masson-Delmotte, V. et al. (eds.), *Global Warming of 1.5°C. An IPCC Special Report on the impacts of global warming of 1.5°C above pre-industrial levels and related global greenhouse gas emission pathways, in the context of strengthening the global response to the threat of climate.....* [22]

Ipsos (2021), *Perils of Perception: Climate Change*, https://www.ipsos.com/en/ipsos-perils-perception-climate-change (accessed on 11 October 2023). [36]

ISSP (2020), *ISSP 2020 "Environment IV" - ZA No. 7650*, https://www.gesis.org/en/issp/data-and-documentation/environment/2020 (accessed on 28 August 2024). [31]

Ivanova, D. et al. (2020), "Quantifying the potential for climate change mitigation of consumption options", *Environmental Research Letters*, Vol. 15/9, p. 093001, https://doi.org/10.1088/1748-9326/ab8589. [7]

Jacob, W. (2015), "Interdisciplinary trends in higher education", *Palgrave Communications*, https://doi.org/10.1057/palcomms.2015.1. [100]

Jensen, B. (2002), "Knowledge, Action and Pro-environmental Behaviour", *Environmental Education Research*, Vol. 8/3, pp. 325-334, https://doi.org/10.1080/13504620220145474. [73]

Khatibi, F. et al. (2021), "Can public awareness, knowledge and engagement improve climate change adaptation policies?", *Discover Sustainability*, Vol. 2/1, https://doi.org/10.1007/s43621-021-00024-z. [10]

KNAW (2022), *Science Communication by Scientists: Rewarded!*, Royal Netherlands Academy of Arts and Sciences (KNAW), https://www.knaw.nl/en/publications/science-communication-scientists-rewarded (accessed on 22 June 2023). [154]

Kormos, C., R. Gifford and E. Brown (2014), "The Influence of Descriptive Social Norm Information on Sustainable Transportation Behavior", *Environment and Behavior*, Vol. 47/5, pp. 479-501, https://doi.org/10.1177/0013916513520416. [138]

Lancaster University (n.d.), *Morecambe Bay Curriculum*, https://www.lancaster.ac.uk/morecambe-bay-curriculum/ (accessed on 5 May 2023). [88]

Lausselet, N. and I. Zosso (2022), "Outdoor and Sustainability Education: How to Link and Implement Them in Teacher Education? An Empirical Perspective", in *Sustainable Development Goals Series, Competences in Education for Sustainable Development*, Springer International Publishing, Cham, https://doi.org/10.1007/978-3-030-91055-6_20. [75]

Lawson, D. et al. (2019), *Children can foster climate change concern among their parents*, Nature Publishing Group, https://doi.org/10.1038/s41558-019-0463-3. [21]

Lawson, H. and D. Veen (2016), "A planning framework for the five core components", in *Developing Community Schools, Community Learning Centers, Extended-service Schools and Multi-service Schools*, Springer. [117]

Lehtonen, A., A. Salonen and H. Cantell (2018), "Climate Change Education: A New Approach for a World of Wicked Problems", in *Sustainability, Human Well-Being, and the Future of Education*, Springer International Publishing, Cham, https://doi.org/10.1007/978-3-319-78580-6_11. [74]

Lempert, R. (2019), "Robust Decision Making (RDM)", in *Decision Making under Deep Uncertainty*, Springer International Publishing, Cham, https://doi.org/10.1007/978-3-030-05252-2_2. [58]

Liebe, U., J. Gewinner and A. Diekmann (2021), "Large and persistent effects of green energy defaults in the household and business sectors", *Nature Human Behaviour*, Vol. 5/5, pp. 576-585, https://doi.org/10.1038/s41562-021-01070-3. [139]

Lochner, J., A. Stechemesser and L. Wenz (2024), "Climate summits and protests have a strong impact on climate change media coverage in Germany", *Communications Earth & Environment*, Vol. 5/1, https://doi.org/10.1038/s43247-024-01434-3. [42]

Marinoni, G., H. Van't Land and T. Jensen (2020), *The Impact of COVID-19 on Higher Education Around the World: IAU Global Survey Report*, International Association of Universities (IAU), Paris, https://www.iau-aiu.net/IMG/pdf/iau_covid19_and_he_survey_report_final_may_2020.pdf (accessed on 9 June 2023). [151]

McGrath, J. (2023), "What systematic connections should we have around schools to support the work of teachers?: Global lessons and the potential of ambition loops", *OECD Education Working Papers*, No. 296, OECD Publishing, Paris, https://doi.org/10.1787/77de597c-en. [115]

McInerney, P., J. Smyth and B. Down (2011), "'Coming to a<i>place</i>near you?' The politics and possibilities of a critical pedagogy of place-based education", *Asia-Pacific Journal of Teacher Education*, Vol. 39/1, pp. 3-16, https://doi.org/10.1080/1359866x.2010.540894. [77]

McLaren, D. et al. (2024), "Developing a minifesta for effective academic-activist collaboration in the context of the climate emergency", *Frontiers in Education*, Vol. 9, https://doi.org/10.3389/feduc.2024.1384614. [144]

Mehleb, R., G. Kallis and C. Zografos (2021), "A discourse analysis of yellow-vest resistance against carbon taxes", *Environmental Innovation and Societal Transitions*, Vol. 40, pp. 382-394, https://doi.org/10.1016/j.eist.2021.08.005. [47]

Ministry of Education and Culture (2022), *Teacher Education Development Programme 2022–2026*, https://julkaisut.valtioneuvosto.fi/bitstream/handle/10024/164179/TeacherEducationDevelopmentProgramme.pdf?sequence=1&isAllowed=y (accessed on 28 August 2024). [112]

Moely, B., A. Furco and J. Reed (2008), "Charity and Social Change: The Impact of Individual Preferences on Service-Learning Outcomes.", *Michigan Journal of Community Service Learning*, Vol. 15/1. [78]

Molderez, I. and E. Fonseca (2018), "The efficacy of real-world experiences and service learning for fostering competences for sustainable development in higher education", *Journal of Cleaner Production*, Vol. 172, pp. 4397-4410, https://doi.org/10.1016/j.jclepro.2017.04.062. [79]

Molthan-Hill, P. et al. (2019), "Climate change education for universities: A conceptual framework from an international study", *Journal of Cleaner Production*, Vol. 226, pp. 1092-1101, https://doi.org/10.1016/j.jclepro.2019.04.053. [125]

Munro, D. (2019), *Skills, training and lifelong learning*, Public Policy Forum. [163]

National Academies of Sciences, Engineering, and Medicine (2018), *How People Learn II*, National Academies Press, Washington, D.C., https://doi.org/10.17226/24783. [76]

NCCA (2024), *Background paper and brief for the development of Leaving Certificate Climate Action and Sustainable Development*, https://ncca.ie/media/5920/background-paper-for-lc-casd_0622.pdf (accessed on 5 December 2024). [95]

NCCA (2024), *Draft Leaving Certificate Climate Action & Sustainable Development specification*, https://ncca.ie/media/whbpljhf/consultation-report-on-draft-specification-for-leaving-certificate-casd.pdf (accessed on 5 December 2024). [94]

NCCA (2024), *Report on the consultation on the draft specification for Leaving Certificate Climate Action and Sustainable Development*, https://ncca.ie/media/whbpljhf/consultation-report-on-draft-specification-for-leaving-certificate-casd.pdf (accessed on 5 December 2024). [93]

NCCPE (n.d.), *National Co-Ordinating Centre for Public Engagement*, https://www.publicengagement.ac.uk/ (accessed on 22 August 2024). [157]

Nobel Prize Outreach (2024), *Scientific thinking for all: A toolkit*, https://www.nobelprize.org/scientific-thinking-for-all/ (accessed on 4 September 2024). [53]

Norwegian Education Directorate (2020), *Core Curriculum: Interdisciplinary Topics*, Norwegian Directorate of Education and Skills, https://www.udir.no/lk20/overordnet-del/prinsipper-for-laring-utvikling-og-danning/tverrfaglige-temaer/?lang=eng (accessed on 30 May 2023). [92]

Nusche, D. (2016), "Student assessment and its relationship with curriculum, teaching and learning in the twenty-first century", in *The SAGE Handbook of Curriculum, Pedagogy and Assessment*, SAGE Publications Ltd, 1 Oliver's Yard, 55 City Road London EC1Y 1SP , https://doi.org/10.4135/9781473921405. [159]

Nusche, D., M. Fuster Rabella and S. Lauterbach (2024), "Rethinking education in the context of climate change: Leverage points for transformative change", *OECD Education Working Papers*, No. 307, OECD Publishing, Paris, https://doi.org/10.1787/f14c8a81-en. [13]

Ockwell, D., L. Whitmarsh and S. O'Neill (2009), "Reorienting Climate Change Communication for Effective Mitigation", *Science Communication*, Vol. 30/3, pp. 305-327, https://doi.org/10.1177/1075547008328969. [129]

OECD (2024), *Constructing scenarios for the future of teaching in Flanders*, Forthcoming. [122]

OECD (2024), "Cultivating the next generation of green and digital innovators: The role of higher education", *OECD Education Policy Perspectives*, No. 95, OECD Publishing, Paris, https://doi.org/10.1787/bb6e432e-en. [91]

OECD (2024), *Education at a Glance 2024: OECD Indicators*, OECD Publishing, Paris, https://doi.org/10.1787/c00cad36-en. [34]

OECD (2024), *OECD Survey on Drivers of Trust in Public Institutions – 2024 Results: Building Trust in a Complex Policy Environment*, OECD Publishing, Paris, https://doi.org/10.1787/9a20554b-en. [26]

OECD (2024), *What Does Child Empowerment Mean Today?: Implications for Education and Well-being*, Educational Research and Innovation, OECD Publishing, Paris, https://doi.org/10.1787/8f80ce38-en. [27]

OECD (2023), "Education and innovation for the digital and green transitions: How higher education can support effective curricula in schools", *OECD Education Policy Perspectives*, https://doi.org/10.1787/5cc2d673-en. [82]

OECD (2023), "Education and innovation for the digital and green transitions: How higher education can support effective curricula in schools", *OECD Education Policy Perspectives*, No. 81, OECD Publishing, Paris, https://doi.org/10.1787/3dedf4cb-en. [52]

OECD (2023), "Education and innovation for the digital and green transitions: How higher education can support teachers and school leaders", *OECD Education Policy Perspectives No. 82* OECD Publishing, Paris, https://doi.org/10.1787/6407e9f4-en (accessed on 6 August 2024). [87]

OECD (2023), *Education Policy Outlook 2023: Empowering All Learners to Go Green*, OECD Publishing, Paris, https://doi.org/10.1787/f5063653-en. [81]

OECD (2023), *Global Science Forum - Responsible communication of science to the public - Workshop summary report*, https://one.oecd.org/document/DSTI/STP/GSF(2023)12/FINAL/en/pdf (accessed on 22 August 2024). [148]

OECD (2023), *How Green is Household Behaviour?: Sustainable Choices in a Time of Interlocking Crises*, OECD Studies on Environmental Policy and Household Behaviour, OECD Publishing, Paris, https://doi.org/10.1787/2bbbb663-en. [32]

OECD (2023), “Implementation of Ireland’s Leaving Certificate 2020-2021: Lessons from the COVID-19 Pandemic”, *OECD Education Policy Perspectives*, No. 73, OECD Publishing, Paris, https://doi.org/10.1787/e36a10b8-en. [96]

OECD (2023), *OECD Skills Outlook 2023: Skills for a Resilient Green and Digital Transition*, OECD Publishing, Paris, https://doi.org/10.1787/27452f29-en. [12]

OECD (2023), “Strengthening higher education-school partnerships for green and digital innovation”, *OECD Education Spotlights No. 8* OECD Publishing, Paris, https://doi.org/10.1787/a77c0d5d-en (accessed on 22 August 2024). [150]

OECD (2022), *Are Students Ready to Take on Environmental Challenges?*, PISA, OECD Publishing, Paris, https://doi.org/10.1787/8abe655c-en. [19]

OECD (2022), *Building Trust and Reinforcing Democracy: Preparing the Ground for Government Action*, OECD Public Governance Reviews, OECD Publishing, Paris, https://doi.org/10.1787/76972a4a-en. [23]

OECD (2021), *Education Policy Outlook 2021: Shaping Responsive and Resilient Education in a Changing World*, OECD Publishing, Paris, https://doi.org/10.1787/75e40a16-en. [25]

OECD (2021), “Think green: Education and climate change”, *Trends Shaping Education Spotlights*, No. 24, OECD Publishing, Paris, https://doi.org/10.1787/2a9a1cdd-en. [103]

OECD (2020), *Curriculum Overload: A Way Forward*, OECD Publishing, Paris, https://doi.org/10.1787/3081ceca-en. [89]

OECD (2019), *Benchmarking Higher Education System Performance*, Higher Education, OECD Publishing, Paris, https://doi.org/10.1787/be5514d7-en (accessed on 28 July 2023). [85]

OECD (2019), *Conceptual Learning Framework: Learning Compass 2030*, OECD Future of Education and Skills 2030, http://www.oecd.org/education/2030-project. [28]

OECD (2019), “OECD Future of Education and Skills 2030: STUDENT AGENCY FOR 2030”, https://www.oecd.org/education/2030-project/teaching-and-learning/learning/student-agency/Student_Agency_for_2030_concept_note.pdf (accessed on 14 June 2024). [24]

OECD (2019), *SSES Round 1 Database*, https://www.oecd.org/en/data/datasets/SSES-Round-1-Database.html (accessed on 6 December 2024). [37]

OECD (2019), *TALIS 2018 Results (Volume I): Teachers and School Leaders as Lifelong Learners*, TALIS, OECD Publishing, Paris, https://doi.org/10.1787/1d0bc92a-en. [98]

OECD (2013), *Synergies for Better Learning: An International Perspective on Evaluation and Assessment*, OECD Reviews of Evaluation and Assessment in Education, OECD Publishing, Paris, https://doi.org/10.1787/9789264190658-en. [97]

Ojala, M. (2016), *Young people and global climate change: Emotions, coping, and engagement in everyday life*, Springer, https://doi.org/10.1007/978-981-4585-54-5_3. [66]

Okada, A. and P. Gray (2023), “A Climate Change and Sustainability Education Movement: Networks, Open Schooling, and the ‘CARE-KNOW-DO’ Framework”, *Sustainability*, Vol. 15/3, p. 2356, https://doi.org/10.3390/su15032356. [104]

Orgill, M., S. York and J. MacKellar (2019), "Introduction to Systems Thinking for the Chemistry Education Community", *Journal of Chemical Education*, Vol. 96/12, pp. 2720-2729, https://doi.org/10.1021/acs.jchemed.9b00169. [55]

Otto, I. (ed.) (2022), ""How dare you?"—The normative challenge posed by Fridays for Future", *PLOS Climate*, Vol. 1/10, p. e0000053, https://doi.org/10.1371/journal.pclm.0000053. [18]

OXFAM (2020), *Confronting Carbon Inequality - Putting climate justice at the heart of the COVID-19 recovery*, https://oxfamilibrary.openrepository.com/bitstream/handle/10546/621052/mb-confronting-carbon-inequality-210920-en.pdf (accessed on 30 August 2024). [49]

Pereira, T. and T. Freire (2021), *Positive Youth Development in the Context of Climate Change: A Systematic Review*, Frontiers Media S.A., https://doi.org/10.3389/fpsyg.2021.786119. [14]

Pfrommer, T. et al. (2019), "Establishing causation in climate litigation: admissibility and reliability", *Climatic Change*, Vol. 152/1, pp. 67-84, https://doi.org/10.1007/s10584-018-2362-4. [146]

Piao, X. and S. Managi (2023), "The international role of education in sustainable lifestyles and economic development", *Scientific Reports*, Vol. 13/1, https://doi.org/10.1038/s41598-023-35173-w. [140]

Pörtner, H. et al. (2022), "Technical Summary", in H.-O. Pörtner et al. (eds.), *Climate Change 2022: Impacts, Adaptation, and Vulnerability. Contribution of Working Group II to the Sixth Assessment Report of the Intergovernmental Panel on Climate Change*, Cambridge University Press. [9]

Price, E. et al. (2022), "Factors associated with nature connectedness in school-aged children", *Current Research in Ecological and Social Psychology*, Vol. 3, p. 100037, https://doi.org/10.1016/j.cresp.2022.100037. [39]

Pye, M. (n.d.), *Next Level Climate Thinking and Action: The Student Guide*. [168]

RCUK (2020), *Engaging Young People with Cutting-Edge Research: A Guide for Researchers and Teachers*, Research Council UK, https://www.ukri.org/wp-content/uploads/2020/10/UKRI-16102020-Schools-Policy.pdf (accessed on 4 April 2023). [153]

Roeser, F. et al. (2023), *Five major shifts since the Paris Agreement that give hope in a just, Paris-compatible transition*, NewClimate Institute, https://newclimate.org/sites/default/files/2023-11/five_major_shifts_since_the_paris_agreement_nov2023.pdf (accessed on 14 June 2024). [17]

Rogelj, J. et al. (2018), "Mitigation Pathways Compatible with 1.5°C in the Context of Sustainable Development", in Masson-Delmotte V. et al. (eds.), *Global Warming of 1.5°C. An IPCC Special Report on the impacts of global warming of 1.5°C above pre-industrial levels and related global greenhouse gas emission pathways, in the context of strengthening the global response to the threat of climate [...]*. [5]

Rousell, D. and A. Cutter-Mackenzie-Knowles (2019), "A systematic review of climate change education: giving children and young people a 'voice' and a 'hand' in redressing climate change", *Children's Geographies*, Vol. 18/2, pp. 191-208, https://doi.org/10.1080/14733285.2019.1614532. [158]

Sato M et al. (2023), *Impacts of climate litigation on firm value.*, Centre for Climate Change Economics and Policy Working Paper 421/Grantham Research Institute on Climate Change and the Environment Working Paper 397. London: London School of Economics and Political Science. [11]

Schubert, C. (2017), "Green nudges: Do they work? Are they ethical?", *Ecological Economics*, Vol. 132, pp. 329-342, https://doi.org/10.1016/j.ecolecon.2016.11.009. [136]

Schultz, W., A. Khazian and A. Zaleski (2008), "Using normative social influence to promote conservation among hotel guests", *Social Influence*, Vol. 3/1, pp. 4-23, https://doi.org/10.1080/15534510701755614. [137]

Schumer, R. and C. Cook (1999), "The Status of Service-Learning in the United States: Some Facts and Figures", *Service Learning, General*, Vol. 144, https://digitalcommons.unomaha.edu/cgi/viewcontent.cgi?article=1143&context=slceslgen&httpsredir=1&referer= (accessed on 22 August 2024). [160]

Schweizer, S., S. Davis and J. Thompson (2013), "Changing the Conversation about Climate Change: A Theoretical Framework for Place-Based Climate Change Engagement", *Environmental Communication*, Vol. 7/1, pp. 42-62, https://doi.org/10.1080/17524032.2012.753634. [72]

Secretary of the Nordic Council of Ministers and Nordic Council of Ministers (2021), *Mapping Education for Sustainability in the Nordic Countries*, Nordic Co-Operation, https://www.norden.org/en/publication/mapping-education-sustainability-nordic-countries (accessed on 9 March 2023). [101]

Segerberg, A. (2017), *Online and Social Media Campaigns For Climate Change Engagement*, Oxford University Press, https://doi.org/10.1093/acrefore/9780190228620.013.398. [130]

Seleviciute, A. and A. Sturlyte (2021), *With art protest, concerned students raise climate alarm*, https://news-decoder.com/with-art-protest-concerned-students-raise-climate-alarm/ (accessed on 5 December 2024). [64]

Setzer J and Higham C (2024), *Global Trends in Climate Change Litigation: 2024 Snapshot*, Grantham Research Institute on Climate Change and the Environment, London School of Economics and Political Science, https://www.lse.ac.uk/granthaminstitute/wp-content/uploads/2024/06/Global-trends-in-climate-change-litigation-2024-snapshot.pdf (accessed on 3 October 2024). [147]

Simac, J., R. Marcus and C. Harper (2019), "Does non-formal education have lasting effects?", *Compare: A Journal of Comparative and International Education*, Vol. 51/5, pp. 706-724, https://doi.org/10.1080/03057925.2019.1669011. [128]

Sipos, Y., B. Battisti and K. Grimm (2008), "Achieving transformative sustainability learning: Engaging head, hands and heart", *International Journal of Sustainability in Higher Education*, Vol. 9/1, pp. 68-86, https://doi.org/10.1108/14676370810842193. [169]

Song, G. and Z. Wang (2021), "Factors influencing middle school students' interdisciplinary competence in science education", *Journal of Research in Science Teaching*, Vol. 58/7, pp. 1041-1072. [119]

Stuart-Smith, R. et al. (2021), "Filling the evidentiary gap in climate litigation", *Nature Climate Change*, Vol. 11/8, pp. 651-655, https://doi.org/10.1038/s41558-021-01086-7. [145]

Tasiopoulou et al (2022), *European Integrated STEM Teaching Framework*, European Schoolnet, Brussels. [109]

The Climate Academy (n.d.), *The Climate Academy*, https://theclimateacademy.org/ (accessed on 17 September 2024). [63]

The Teaching Council (2020), *Céim: Standards for Initial Teacher Education*, https://www.teachingcouncil.ie/assets/uploads/2023/08/ceim-standards-for-initial-teacher-education.pdf (accessed on 28 August 2024). [111]

Tilbury, D. and C. Galvin (2022), *Input paper: A whole school approach to learning for environmental sustainability*, Publications Office of the European Union, Luxembourg, https://education.ec.europa.eu/document/input-paper-a-whole-school-approach-to-learning-for-environmental-sustainability (accessed on 4 April 2023). [70]

UBU (2022), *PÅ VEJ MOD UDDANNELSER FOR BÆREDYGTIG UDVIKLING*, Government of Denmark, https://verdensmaalene.cdn.prismic.io/verdensmaalene/0f0df43a-2e4a-463e-bc4d-5af1330bf793_UBU_rapport_sept22.pdf (accessed on 9 March 2023). [102]

Valentim, A. (2023), *Repeated Exposure and Protest Outcomes: How Fridays for Future Protests Influenced Voters*, Center for Open Science, https://doi.org/10.31235/osf.io/m6dpg. [44]

VIBGYOR Group of Schools (2024), , https://www.instagram.com/reel/C5lOm5cPIU4/?igsh=MW53amhtZTA0a3FyNw%3D%3D (accessed on 5 December 2024). [65]

von Stechow, C. et al. (2015), "Integrating Global Climate Change Mitigation Goals with Other Sustainability Objectives: A Synthesis", *Annual Review of Environment and Resources*, Vol. 40/1, pp. 363-394, https://doi.org/10.1146/annurev-environ-021113-095626. [4]

Voulvoulis, N. et al. (2022), "Systems thinking as a paradigm shift for sustainability transformation", *Global Environmental Change*, Vol. 75, p. 102544, https://doi.org/10.1016/j.gloenvcha.2022.102544. [56]

Wang, H. et al. (2020), "Defining interdisciplinary collaboration based on high school teachers' beliefs and practices of STEM integration using a complex designed system", *International Journal of STEM Education*, Vol. 7/1, p. 3, https://doi.org/10.1186/s40594-019-0201-4. [120]

Werfel, S. (2017), "Household behaviour crowds out support for climate change policy when sufficient progress is perceived", *Nature Climate Change*, Vol. 7/7, pp. 512-515, https://doi.org/10.1038/nclimate3316. [167]

Werquin, P. (2010), *Recognising Non-Formal and Informal Learning: Outcomes, Policies and Practices*, OECD Publishing, Paris, https://doi.org/10.1787/9789264063853-en. [127]

White, P. et al. (2023), *Agency in the Anthropocene : Supporting document to the PISA 2025 Science Framework | OECD Education Working Papers | OECD iLibrary*, https://www.oecd-ilibrary.org/education/agency-in-the-anthropocene_8d3b6cfa-en (accessed on 3 October 2023). [29]

Wissenschaft im Dialog (n.d.), *Wissenschaft im Dialog [Science in Dialogue]*, https://www.wissenschaft-im-dialog.de/ (accessed on 22 June 2023). [155]

Wynes, S. and K. Nicholas (2017), "The climate mitigation gap: Education and government recommendations miss the most effective individual actions", *Environmental Research Letters*, Vol. 12/7, https://doi.org/10.1088/1748-9326/aa7541. [15]

Youngs, R. (2024), *Is There a Silver Lining to Europe's Climate Change Turmoil?*, https://carnegieendowment.org/research/2024/02/is-there-a-silver-lining-to-europes-climate-change-turmoil?lang=en&center=europe (accessed on 4 September 2024). [48]

Zen, I. (2017), "Exploring the living learning laboratory: An approach to strengthen campus sustainability initiatives by using sustainability science approach", *International Journal of Sustainability in Higher Education*, Vol. 18/6, https://www.emerald.com/insight/content/doi/10.1108/IJSHE-09-2015-0154/full/html. [161]

Notes

1 The Anthropocene, or the Age of Humans, is the name proposed by a range of scientists to refer to the geological epoch in which human activity is fundamentally altering Earth systems and life-sustaining processes on the planet, as evidenced in the geological record and directly experienced through the earth's changing climate.

2 In PISA, a student's socio-economic background is estimated using the PISA index of economic, social, and cultural status. This composite measure combines financial, social, cultural, and human capital resources available to students into a single score.

3 While offering interesting illustrations, it should be noted that these test items do not offer sufficient information to construct an overall index of students' environmental science proficiency. An index measuring students' proficiency in environmental sciences will become available as part of the PISA 2025 results, to be published in 2026.

4 More information on students' behavioural choices and environmental actions will become available with the PISA 2025 results, to be published in 2026.

5 Being "environmentally enthusiastic" is defined as being aware of climate change and global warming, expressing high levels of self-efficacy with respect to their environmental science knowledge and reporting that looking after the environment is important to them.

6 SSES was conducted in 10 cities internationally, of which eight are located in OECD countries.

7 The survey was conducted in Australia, Canada, United Kingdom, United States, Finland, Germany, Italy, Norway, China, Hong Kong, Malaysia, Argentina, Brazil.

3 Building a strategic vision for skills development for the green transition

Achieving a sustainable future requires policies that ensure long-term employment and social well-being, presenting both challenges and opportunities for policymakers working to transition job markets toward greener economies. This ever-changing landscape requires a workforce that is well-prepared with the necessary skills, highlighting the crucial role of education in equipping individuals to meet the demands of sustainable markets and jobs.

In their Declaration on Building Equitable Societies Through Education in 2022, OECD Education Ministers called on the OECD's Education Policy Committee (EDPC) and other OECD Committees to support countries in building "a new vision for skills development that keeps pace with changes in societies and economies and supports the transition to net zero" and in developing "strategies to empower and support all learners appropriately to build foundational and transferable skills for current and future labour markets as well as for digital and green democracies" (OECD, 2022[1]).

The shift to an inclusive green economy is a powerful engine for growth and has the potential to create quality employment—characterised by e.g. fair wages, job security, safe working conditions—across developing, emerging, and advanced economies (van der Ree, 2019[2]). This chapter will explore the role of education in supporting the green transition of economies and labour markets, from a perspective of skills development. Based on a review of a wide range of OECD publications and additional evidence, it will first examine the concrete implications of the green transition for labour markets and skills needs in a changing world. Secondly, the chapter will explore the role of education in promoting skills development in line with current and anticipated labour-market changes brought about by the green transition.

The evolving labour-market landscape in the green transition

A snapshot of labour-market changes

The policies countries are adopting globally to achieve net-zero greenhouse gas (GHG) emissions by 2050 will significantly impact labour markets by reducing jobs in high-emission industries, creating new opportunities in climate-friendly sectors, and transforming many existing occupations. Much attention has been paid to the impact of the green transition on the quantity of jobs, *i.e.* whether it will create more or fewer jobs than those that it will destroy. While estimates vary, there is broad agreement that the net effect of the transition on the number of jobs will be relatively modest (OECD, 2024[3]).

While the total number of jobs may not be significantly impacted by the transition, profound changes in the composition of jobs and significant shifts within and across sectors and regions are expected. The Employment Outlook 2024 finds that around 20% of workers in OECD countries are currently employed in green-driven occupations, as opposed to 7% in GHG-intensive occupations. It is important to note that the

Employment Outlook 2024 uses a broad definition of green-driven occupations, which includes "all jobs that are likely to be affected by the net-zero transition and not just those that may be considered green as such" (OECD, 2024[3]) (for more detail on definitions, see Box 3.1).

Overall, among green-driven occupations, the category of "green new and emerging jobs", i.e. previously non-existent jobs with unique new tasks and worker requirements (see Box 3.1 for definitions), has seen the fastest growth over the last decade, with their share increasing by some 13% in European OECD countries and the United States during that period. According to global LinkedIn job postings, the proportion of green talent (defined by LinkedIn as those workers with green jobs or who list at least one green skill on their LinkedIn profile) in the global workforce increased by a median of 12.3% between 2022 and 2023 and job postings demanding at least one green skill grew at double that rate (LinkedIn, 2024[4]). Between 2011 and 2022, while the share of GHG-intensive occupations declined by 18%, the share of green-driven occupations in overall employment increased by 2%, (OECD, 2024[3]).

Box 3.1. Definitions

To analyse green labour-market transitions, it is essential to define what is meant by different job types—specifically, which are considered green, polluting and neutral. Defining green jobs is challenging, with no universally accepted definition, posing ongoing difficulties for policymakers. Different definitions emphasise various aspects of the transition. Top-down approaches define green jobs broadly within sectors or activities contributing to environmental goals, using process-based or output-based methods. Bottom-up approaches identify green jobs based on specific tasks or keywords in job descriptions, offering a more detailed, occupation-specific perspective. This report primarily uses the "green-driven occupations" definition from the OECD Employment Outlook 2024 (OECD, 2024[3]), but mostly refers to "green-task jobs" when discussing regional labour-market differences, based on definitions from *Job Creation and Local Economic Development 2023* (OECD, 2023[5]).

Green-driven occupations

Green-driven occupations are defined as "all jobs that are likely to be affected by the net-zero transition and not just those that may be considered green as such". Green-driven occupations comprise "green new and emerging occupations" (new occupations with unique tasks and worker requirements), "green-enhanced skills occupations" (existing occupations whose skill set is being altered because of the green transition), and "green increased demand occupations" (existing jobs that will be in demand because they provide goods and services required by green activities) (OECD, 2024[3]).

Green-task jobs

Green-task jobs are defined as jobs with a considerable share of green tasks (at least 10%) that directly help to improve environmental sustainability or reduce greenhouse gas emissions (OECD, 2023[5]).

GHG-intensive industries and occupations

High-emission industries are defined as those with the highest greenhouse gas emissions based on data from several European countries between 2009 and 2020. These industries are identified by ranking them according to their emissions, with the top 20% being labelled as high-emission. Together, these industries account for at least 70% of greenhouse gas emissions in each OECD country for which data are available. Jobs within these high-emission industries are identified as greenhouse gas-intensive occupations. This approach helps ensure consistency across different countries and aligns with models predicting the impact of environmental policies. (OECD, 2024[3]).

Neutral occupations

Neutral occupations refer to jobs that are neither green-driven nor GHG-intensive and thus not directly associated with the green transition (OECD, 2024[3]).

Note: For an in-depth methodological discussion of approaches, refer to (Causa, Nguyen and Soldani, 2024[6]) "Lost in the green transition? Measurement and stylized facts", *OECD Economics Department Working Papers*, No. 1796, OECD Publishing, Paris, https://doi.org/10.1787/dce1d5fe-en.
Source: (OECD, 2024[3]) OECD Employment Outlook 2024: The Net-Zero Transition and the Labour Market, OECD Publishing, Paris, https://doi.org/10.1787/ac8b3538-en; (OECD, 2023[5]) Job Creation and Local Economic Development 2023: Bridging the Great Green Divide, OECD Publishing, Paris, https://doi.org/10.1787/21db61c1-en.

When it comes to job quality, green-driven occupations generally offer higher wages and fewer temporary contracts than other occupations; at the same time, they often come with a higher risk of unemployment. But these occupations encompass a diverse range of jobs—from high-skill positions such as managers, professionals, and engineers to medium—and low-skill roles employing many workers with low educational attainment levels. The quality of these jobs often varies based on the skill levels required. The quality advantage of green-driven occupations is mainly seen in high-skill roles, where workers with the necessary competencies have a competitive edge. In contrast, low-skill green-driven jobs tend to offer lower wages and less job security than other low-skill occupations (OECD, 2024[3]).

GHG-intensive occupations, found mainly in high-emission industries, make up only 7% of overall employment across the OECD. While these jobs often offer relatively good wages, they also tend to have a higher incidence of low wages and poorer working conditions. Although these roles do not currently have larger unemployment risks than other occupations, employment in these sectors is projected to decrease by over 2% every year between 2019 and 2030, compared to a 1% annual decline since the 2000s. This rapid contraction is likely to significantly increase the risk of job displacement in high-emission industries (OECD, 2024[3]).

As the demand for green-driven occupations continues to rise, challenges to meet this demand are also increasing. It is important to consider a broader context in which labour markets remain tight (OECD, 2023[7]). Across the 19 OECD countries with available data, the number of vacancies per unemployed person has decreased from its 2021 peak but remains significantly higher than pre-COVID-19 levels. In the coming years, several countries and employment sectors are likely to face qualified labour shortages (International Labour Organization, 2023[8]).

The European Commission (EC) projects that the green transition will create one million new jobs until 2030, and finds that labour shortages already doubled between 2015 and 2021 in key green sectors and jobs (European Commission, 2023[9]). Indeed, 85% of European firms state that the lack of available skills delays crucial investments in long-term structural challenges like the climate transition (European Investment Bank (EIB), 2023[10]). A 2024 analysis of key sectors in ten countries across the Global North and Global South concludes that the supply of skilled workers is unlikely to meet the demand (Sam Huckstep and Helen Dempster, 2024[11]).

These critical shortages not only risk slowing down progress towards global environmental goals but may also exacerbate inequalities in local labour markets if there is insufficient attention to ensuring that all workers can benefit from the new job opportunities brought by the green transition (OECD, 2024[3]). Analyses converge to show that the green transition is generating and will continue to generate high-quality jobs, but that these are primarily concentrated in high-skill occupations.

While green-driven occupations present significant opportunities for highly educated workers with the necessary competencies, they may not appeal as much to low-skilled workers compared to jobs in high-emission industries. This underscores the need for measures to enhance the quality of green-driven employment, especially in low-skilled jobs, and highlights the critical role of public policies in supporting the transition, such as upskilling initiatives and other labour market interventions. Ensuring a just transition is essential, where the benefits and opportunities of the green economy are accessible to all workers and all regions, and those at risk of job displacement are adequately supported through targeted re-skilling and social protection measures (Box 3.2).

Box 3.2. Just transition and skills

As the global transition to net-zero GHG emissions continues and accelerates, and economies and societies transform to be aligned with climate goals, a key priority for governments is ensuring a just transition. The net zero transition will naturally entail both opportunities and adverse effects for different segments of populations, with the risk of creating winners and losers. It is essential to ensure that distributional consequences are managed carefully, and both benefits and losses are shared as far as possible. Climate policies should not exacerbate existing inequalities, and particular attention should be paid to marginalised groups, including women and girls, migrants, socioeconomically disadvantaged people. Given the regional concentration of both high-emitting and emerging green occupations, it is equally important to consider the spatial dimensions of equity and ensure that vulnerable regions within countries are not left behind.

In addition, just transition is increasingly being considered not only in terms of equity within countries but also justice between countries. While they have the least responsibility for cumulative GHG emissions, developing countries face extreme challenges in the transition to net-zero emissions (in addition to their frequently high vulnerability to the impacts of climate change itself). Developing countries often face the need to transition their economies while balancing priorities related to formalising the workforce and ensuring energy access, while tackling constraints related to capacity and finance. Recognising this challenging position, there is increasing focus, among both developed and developing countries, for a holistic approach to just transition that considers justice at the global level (OECD, 2024[12]). Given strong linkages with development processes, effective skills policies to support the transition in the energy sector in developing countries are critical, as discussed in Annex A.

The need to ensure a just transition comes not only from ethical concerns, but from fundamental considerations of effectiveness. The success of the green transition depends on its social acceptability. The perceived distributional impacts of climate policies are one of the key factors determining their levels of public support (Dechezleprêtre et al., 2022[13]). Should climate policies unduly burden, or be perceived to unduly burden, certain individuals or groups, they are likely to be socially divisive and to be met with unequal public support, or even social unrest, slowing, halting, or potentially reversing the implementation of climate ambitions. For instance, for every 1% increase in unemployment, the percentage of adults who report prioritising the environment over the economy declines by 1.7% (OECD, 2023[14]). As such, carefully managing the impacts of the transition on populations is essential to ensure the speed and ultimate resilience of the transition to a low-carbon economy.

Among the most visible distributional impacts of the transition are those on jobs and labour markets. As discussed, education is a key driver of individuals' ability to transition into green jobs and to capture the benefits associated with green jobs. Indeed, a region's ability to benefit from the green transition depends significantly on the skills available in its local labour market. Higher shares of scientific, technical and information activities in a given region correlate with a higher share of green-task jobs. The regions with the greatest share of green-task jobs also tend to have a higher share of population with tertiary education (OECD, 2023[5]). This implies the need to incorporate considerations of equity and inclusiveness as education and skills policies increasingly target the preparedness of the workforce for the new green economy. Effective policies in this area can facilitate smooth transitions, lead to improvements in working conditions, and minimise widespread job losses and contractual instability.

These considerations of justice underscore the need to ensure the wide reach of education and skills policies. It is essential to promote skills development among the most vulnerable. However, efforts to date are falling short. As described in Chapter 1, socio-economic status is a significant predictor of environmental sustainability-related educational attainment. Among both teenagers and adults, many disadvantaged groups access career guidance services less frequently. Women continue to be underrepresented in science, technology, engineering and mathematics (STEM) education, which is a powerful predictor of obtaining a job in the green economy (OECD, 2023[14]) (Causa et al., 2024[15]). There is a major gender difference in green-driven occupations, with only 11.5% of women holding a green-driven job, compared to 28.9% of men (OECD, 2024[3]).

As outlined in the OECD Employment Outlook (2024[3]), employees in high-emission sectors, and thus those most at risk of displacement, are predominantly male, older and more likely to live in rural areas than other workers. These workers also tend to be employed in relatively high paying firms (partly due to a higher coverage rate by collective agreements in GHG-intensive occupations) but they have relatively low educational attainment compared to workers in low-emission industries. This combination of worker characteristics means that job displacement in high-emission sectors is likely to be 20% more costly than in other sectors of the economy. Displaced workers in high-emission industries face a decline in annual earnings of 38% on average during the five years since displacement, while displaced workers in low-emission industries face a decline of 31% (OECD, 2024[3]). This highlights the importance of developing a skills delivery landscape that offers attractive, flexible and inclusive provision of upskilling and re-skilling opportunities (see Section on Building a coherent skills delivery landscape for the green transition).

Source: (OECD, 2024[3]) *OECD Employment Outlook 2024: The Net-Zero Transition and the Labour Market*, OECD Publishing, Paris, https://doi.org/10.1787/ac8b3538-en; (OECD, 2023[14]) *OECD Skills Outlook 2023: Skills for a Resilient Green and Digital Transition*, OECD Publishing, Paris, https://doi.org/10.1787/27452f29-en; (Causa et al., 2024[15]) *"Labour markets transitions in the greening economy: Structural drivers and the role of policies"*, OECD Economics Department Working Papers, No. 1803, OECD Publishing, Paris, https://doi.org/10.1787/d8007e8f-en; (OECD, 2024[12]) *Development Co-operation Report 2024: Tackling Poverty and Inequalities through the Green Transition*, OECD Publishing, Paris, https://doi.org/10.1787/357b63f7-en; (Dechezleprêtre et al., 2022[13]) *"Fighting climate change: International attitudes toward climate policies"*, OECD Economics Department Working Papers, No. 1714, OECD Publishing, Paris, https://doi.org/10.1787/3406f29a-en; (OECD, 2023[14]) *OECD Skills Outlook 2023: Skills for a Resilient Green and Digital Transition*, OECD Publishing, Paris, https://doi.org/10.1787/27452f29-en; (OECD, 2023[5]) *Job Creation and Local Economic Development 2023: Bridging the Great Green Divide*, OECD Publishing, Paris, https://doi.org/10.1787/21db61c1-en.

The regional dimension of labour-market changes

While the net-zero transition is a global challenge requiring international and national efforts, its impact on labour market and skills will be felt keenly at local level. Even if aggregate employment effects of the transition at national level are modest, regions will be affected differently by a shift towards greener labour markets. Some will be well poised to take advantage of emerging opportunities, while others stand to be more negatively affected. OECD analysis indicates that to date the share of green-task jobs varies significantly within countries, with an average 7 percentage point difference between the top and bottom regions across the OECD, and capital regions often having the highest share (OECD, 2023[7]; OECD, 2023[5]).

Employment risks tend to be regionally concentrated. In particular, regions with a high share of jobs in high-emissions sectors are more likely to experience job losses. For example, OECD modelling on the effects of the EU's Fit for 55 package indicates that blue-collar workers in the coal and lignite mining sector will be severely impacted. In 2019, most of these workers were concentrated in five countries—Bulgaria,

Czechia, Germany, Poland, and Romania—requiring targeted attention and support (Borgonovi et al., 2023[16]).

Urban-rural location is also a significant factor. Green-driven occupations are a heterogeneous group of jobs and are represented differently in different geographies. Green new and emerging occupations are typically high-skilled and employ highly educated workers in urban areas. It is among these high-skilled jobs that the advantages of green-driven jobs are most concentrated. The other green-driven occupations are on average more medium- and low-skilled and employ many more low-educated workers in rural areas. GHG-intensive occupations also tend to be concentrated in rural areas, but in different regions than green-driven occupations (OECD, 2024[3]). While the transferability of workers' skills is one factor in their possible transition to other industries, geography is likely to be another large barrier. Since workers in GHG-intensive occupations are often not located in the same areas as emerging green jobs, the number of job switches that can occur is limited (Lim, Aklin and Frank, 2023[17]).

In regions with a high concentration of polluting industries adopting green technologies and ways of working can come at a high cost, due to the investments needed not just to adapt existing infrastructure, but also to upskill and reskill the existing workforce. In areas with significant potential for the development of green industries at scale (such as the wind industry in coastal or remote areas), the challenges may lie in attracting a mix of both vocationally and academically trained workers to those areas, which are often sparsely populated, and in significantly scaling up educational opportunities, along with other core services to make those areas more attractive (Grashof and Basilico, 2024[18]). Recent evidence from the OECD shows that, in 31 countries with available data, 66% of people living in remote regions can access tertiary education within a 45-minute car trip, compared with 98% for those living in larger metropolitan areas (OECD, 2023[19]).

Since many rural regions fail to match the standards provided by urban areas, not only in terms of educational opportunities, but also access to healthcare, internet connectivity or high-quality work, many young people and adults move to cities for further education and employment. This trend contributes to widening the urban-rural education gap, which is of growing concern for governments (Teo et al., 2023[20]; Millward, 2023[21]). Between 2012 and 2020, the number of countries where the share of adults (24-65 years-old) with a tertiary degree was higher in urban than rural areas grew from 19 to 25 countries (out of 26 countries with available data). In 2020, the urban-rural gap in tertiary attainment was as wide as 30 percentage points in Hungary, compared with 2 percentage points in Belgium (OECD, 2023[19]). Without policy action, the transition risks leaving those without the necessary skills behind, and deepening divides between regions (OECD, 2023[5]).

Importantly, while the impact of the transition on skills demand and labour markets differs across regions within countries, it also differs significantly between countries, including between developed and developing countries. It is essential for transition planning to consider the specific national contexts and the heterogeneous starting points of different countries. Developing countries have the least responsibility for cumulative GHG emissions (Box 1.3 on Carbon Inequality Chapter 1) but face potentially severe impacts from both climate change and the net-zero transition, exacerbating existing economic challenges. Rapid population growth, urbanisation, and rising energy demand are key trends in many developing countries. Unique challenges persist in developing countries due to diverse labour markets, underfunded welfare and social protection, lower capacity of government and institutions, and technology gaps (OECD, 2022[22]). Moreover, only 1.5% of global climate finance in 2021 was for the education sector (Sabarwal et al., 2024[23]). At the same time, the global transition can also provide key opportunities to developing countries for more sustainable growth and may allow for more workers to transition from informal to formal employment.

Skills requirements for the green transition

As the world shifts towards more sustainable practices, the green transition requires a diverse set of skills to address complex environmental challenges. Numerous frameworks have been developed to outline the essential sustainability competencies (Box 1.7 International frameworks articulating sustainability competencies in Chapter 1) and to describe skills required for transitioning towards a sustainable future. For example, based on the definition of green skills by the European Centre for the Development of Vocational Training (Cedefop)[1] (Cedefop, 2012[24]), the European Skills, Competences, Qualifications and Occupations provides a classification of a range of skills and knowledge concepts as "green"[2] (ESCO, 2022[25]). Various frameworks, while not identical, broadly align on a key set of skills necessary for the green transition. These skills fall in the combination of three broad aspects:

- **Technical skills**: These encompass occupation or sector-specific competencies that demand technical expertise, such as proficiency in production processes, machine operations, and other specialised tasks essential to a particular field or industry.
- **Transversal skills**: Also called transferable skills, these are versatile abilities that can be applied across different jobs, industries, or situations. Examples include communication, teamwork, problem-solving, adaptability, and leadership. These skills are crucial for navigating diverse challenges and tasks, enhancing overall versatility and employability.
- **Sustainability competencies**: These encompass a solid understanding of the interrelationship between social and ecological systems; critical, creative and systems thinking; and a disposition to act and engage with others in shaping a sustainable future (see Chapter 1).

One key finding of the OECD Employment Outlook 2024 is that skills themselves are not intrinsically "green"; their impact depends on how they are applied (OECD, 2024[3]). This is particularly true for transversal skills which are in high demand for roles across green-driven, neutral and GHG-intensive sectors. Indeed, the application of individuals' skills for positive or negative environmental impact depends on the types of jobs they choose and on the way they use their skills in these jobs, which in turn is influenced by their attitudes and dispositions and ultimately by their "sustainability competencies" (see Chapter 1). These attitudes and dispositions are crucial enablers of skill development and investment; skills only lead to meaningful action if accompanied by the will and the opportunities to act (OECD, 2023[14]).

It is important to note that the competencies required to develop agency for socio-behavioural change (explored in Chapter 1) overlap significantly with the skills required for a workforce prepared for the green transition (explored in this chapter), with competencies such as critical thinking, systems thinking and collaborative problem-solving being key for both. However, while these areas share common ground in terms of fostering awareness, skills and competencies related to sustainability, they may diverge in their implications for policy and practice. Education geared towards sustainability and climate action typically focuses on cultivating citizen engagement, promoting advocacy skills, and nurturing a sense of responsibility towards the planet. This approach often calls for policies that support curriculum adaptations, community engagement initiatives, and public awareness campaigns, as explored in Chapter 1.

Conversely, education and training aimed at building a sustainable workforce also prioritises technical skills, and mobilises innovation, systems thinking and entrepreneurship skills that are particularly relevant for green industries and occupations (see also Box 3.4). Policies in this realm may entail investments in vocational education and training, incentives for green innovation hubs, and collaborations between education and training providers and industries to align curricula with emerging environmental needs. While all learning pathways share a common goal of preparing individuals to exercise agency in the context of socio-ecological challenges, their distinct focus underscores the need for holistic skills strategies capable of fostering both individual agency and workforce readiness in the face of environmental crises.

To achieve a sustainable future for all, rapid and far-reaching transitions across all sectors and systems are necessary, with a broad set of technical, transversal and sustainability skills becoming available. First, this section will briefly discuss sector-specific transitions and technical skills requirements, with a deep dive on the energy transition included in Annex A. Second, the section will discuss the transversal or cross-functional skills necessary for the green transition, analysing whether higher levels of these skills are required for green-driven occupations compared to other jobs.[3]

Sector-specific transitions and implications for technical skills demand

While the net effect of the green transition on the number of jobs is likely to be modest, the transition will have major implications for specific sectors and the regions where they are located. Figure 3.1 shows a range of mitigation and adaptation measures and their potential for emissions reductions across different sectors of the economy. Not only will GHG-intensive sectors undergo substantial transformation and green sectors grow, but the green transition will also have a more nuanced impact on jobs and skills needs across the economy, including in sectors that are neither green nor polluting.

Mitigation and adaptation measures across sectors, such as the ones described in Figure 3.1, will have important implications for demand of technical skills in each sector. Interestingly, OECD (2024[3]) finds that technical skills, for example those related to machine operation or maintenance in clean-energy engineering jobs, are *on average* required at lower proficiency levels in green-driven occupations. This does not imply that technical skills are unimportant; in fact, a shortage of these critical technical skills would pose severe obstacles to the transition in all transitioning sectors. Still, the analysis highlights the relatively greater importance of higher levels of proficiency in transversal and analytical skills in the overall skill set required for green-driven occupations (OECD, 2024[3]).

Figure 3.1. Mitigation and adaptation measures in different systems and sectors in line with low-carbon transformation

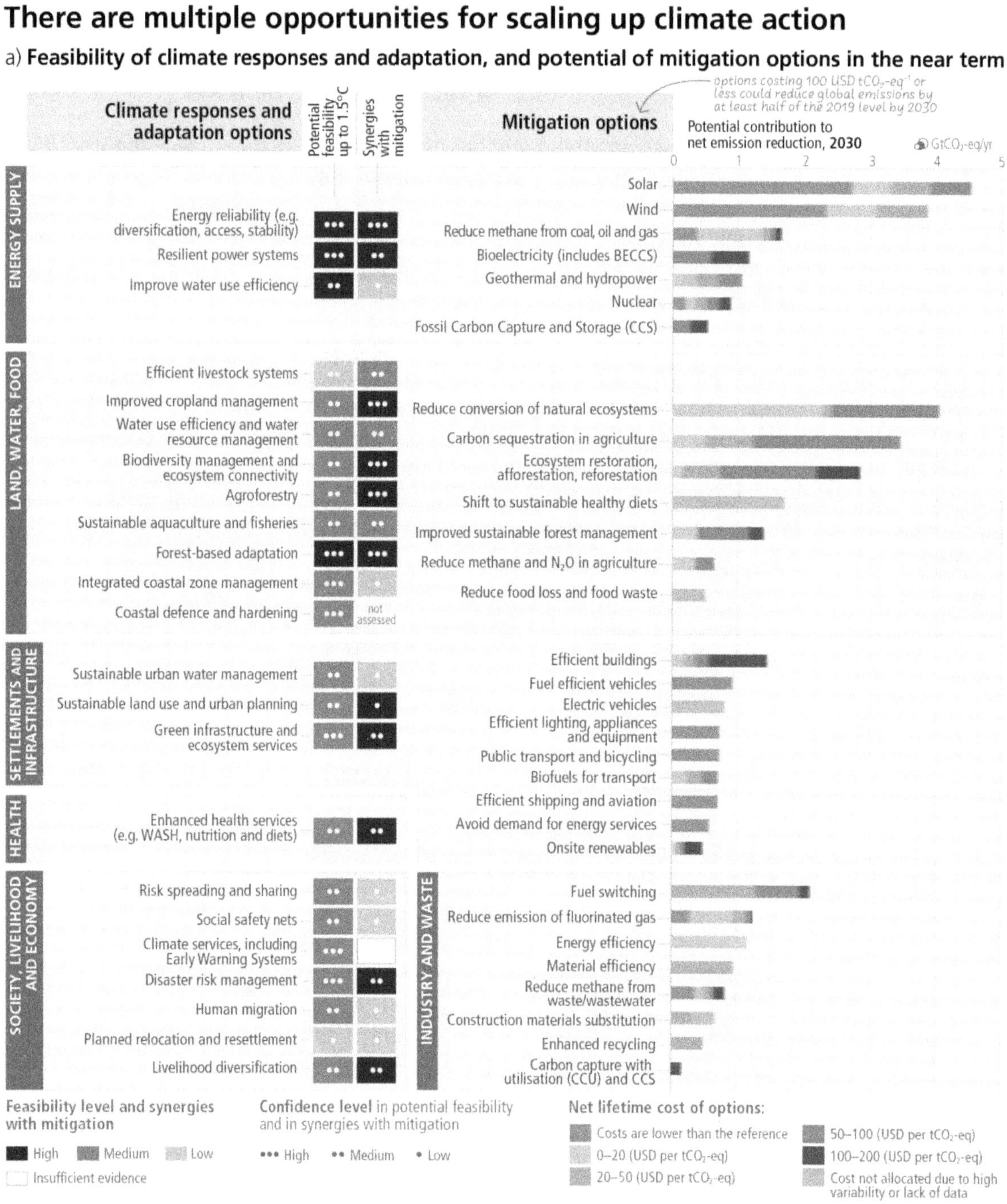

Source: (IPCC, 2023[26]) *Climate Change 2023: Synthesis Report. Contribution of Working Groups I, II and III to the Sixth Assessment Report of the Intergovernmental Panel on Climate Change [Core Writing Team, H. Lee and J. Romero (eds.)]. IPCC, Geneva, Switzerland.*, IPCC, Geneva, Switzerland, https://doi.org/10.59327/IPCC/AR6-9789291691647.

To illustrate the profound changes some economic sectors are undergoing in the context of the green transition, Annex A offers a deep dive on how the demand for technical skills is likely to evolve in the energy sector, which is both a major direct contributor to global GHG emissions and a key area for achieving significant reductions across most sectors of the economy.

Broader transversal skills requirements for the green transition

Accelerating the transition and minimising its cost to workers necessitates a deeper understanding of skill requirements to enhance job transition mechanisms. In that context, it is important to move beyond discussions centred around technical skills for the green transition and look at the wider skill sets required in emerging and in-demand jobs (OECD, 2024[3]). Indeed, as discussed, skills are not inherently "green"; their environmental impact depends on how they are applied, shaped by individuals' attitudes, dispositions, and "sustainability competencies," which are essential for translating skills into meaningful action (Ibid).

Skills identified as critical for green-driven occupations are those transversal process and cross-functional skills linked to the knowledge economy. These include critical thinking, monitoring, active learning, problem-solving, and decision-making, all essential for helping workers adapt to the innovative landscape of the green transition (OECD, 2024[3]). Additionally, fostering system-level resilience to environmental challenges requires empowering individuals to develop information-processing, socio-emotional, and metacognitive abilities (OECD, 2023[14]). Furthermore, skills that promote climate literacy, including foundational skills in literacy, numeracy, and STEM—such as computer literacy and data analysis—will be crucial for the green transition and in particular for the development of high-tech job profiles (see Box 3.3) (OECD, 2023[7]).

Box 3.3. The importance of literacy, numeracy and STEM skills for the green transition: findings from recent econometric analysis

Based on a large sample of European countries over the period 2011-2019, an OECD analysis on labour-market transitions has found that education is the most important individual-level driver of transitions from non-employment to green jobs (using a task-based definition). The odds of getting a green job are twice as high for workers with high levels of education relative to those with low levels of education.

The positive effect is particularly strong for education in science, technology, engineering and mathematics (STEM) for young people entering the labour market. The odds of transitioning to a green occupation are twice as high for young individuals with medium education in STEM relative to those with low education, but also relative to those with non-STEM medium education. Highly educated students with a degree in engineering are most likely to transition to green jobs, with six times higher odds than the low education reference group. Women's odds of transitioning from unemployment to green jobs is 60% relative to men. These results imply a clear role for investing in relevant post-secondary and lifelong learning and a need to remove barriers for women in STEM education (including by combating stereotypes).

Analysis of structural policies found that transitions from non-employment to green jobs are more likely in countries where adults' proficiency in numeracy and literacy is high, and where the incidence of underperforming adults is low. Transitions into green jobs are more likely in countries featuring higher shares of population with tertiary education attainment. Higher shares of government spending allocated to education, not least tertiary education, are associated with higher chances of moving from joblessness to green jobs among women. The estimates suggest that well-developed systems of adults' learning through training and job-related education can help workers seize new opportunities provided by green jobs, particularly in the case of workers with high and medium educational attainments.

Source: (Causa et al., 2024[15]) "Labour markets transitions in the greening economy: Structural drivers and the role of policies", *OECD Economics Department Working Papers*, No. 1803, OECD Publishing, Paris, https://doi.org/10.1787/d8007e8f-en.

This shift in skill demand is also illustrated by OECD modelling analysis, which has examined the economy-wide changes in labour markets and the demand for skills resulting from implementing policies aimed at reducing GHG emissions by considering the case of the European Union's Fit for 55 policy package (OECD, 2023[14]) (Borgonovi et al., 2023[16]). Projections indicate declining labour-market opportunities to 2030 for blue-collar workers and declining demand for skills involving the use of tools and technologies adopted in traditional manufacturing processes. By contrast, the demand for skills related to interacting with computers; thinking creatively; analysing data and information; and communicating with persons outside an organisation is projected to significantly increase by 2030.

Even where there are significant overlaps between the skills needed for green and high-emitting occupations, transitioning from one sector to another is not without challenges for individuals. OECD (2024[3]) offers analysis of the level of preparation required across a range of broad skills (e.g. content, problem-solving, system skills, social skills), comparing the average skill requirements of green-driven, GHG-intensive, and neutral occupations (for definitions, see Box 3.1). The analysis finds that, overall, high-skilled occupations face smaller differences in skill requirements across job categories than low-skilled occupations. This suggests that transitions from GHG-intensive to innovative, green-driven occupations might be easier for high-skilled workers compared to low-skilled workers, who would need significant re-skilling. Low-skilled workers might find transitions to neutral occupations more feasible but still require substantial training to enter green-driven jobs. Without accessible training for all, particularly for the disadvantaged, filling lower-skilled green-driven job vacancies and aiding displaced workers could be challenging, risking their exclusion from the green transition (OECD, 2024[3]) (see Box 3.2 for implications for a just transition).

Conclusions and policy options

Developing skills for high green potential jobs has become crucial in today's workforce as job markets are shifting towards more sustainable economies. Many questions arise for policy makers when navigating this dynamic and ever-evolving landscape. Indeed, policy makers must prioritise the strategic importance of the education and training sector for the transition to greener societies by ensuring fit-for-purpose programmes and learning opportunities for society as a whole to meet the demands of the green labour market (OECD, 2023[7]).

Skills development policies to date are not keeping up with the required pace of change. On average across OECD countries, only around four in ten adults participate in formal or non-formal learning for job-related reasons (OECD, 2021[27]). Workers in green-driven and GHG-intensive occupations participate in training less than those in neutral occupations (OECD, 2024[3]). According to an OECD policy questionnaire, most OECD governments have introduced incentives for education and training institutions to develop or update course content to align with the skills needed for the transition. Some governments have given subsidies or tax deductions to employers offering green-related training to employees. Still, it appears that the current supply of green-related training may be insufficient to meet demand (OECD, 2024, forthcoming[28]).

Analysis from the OECD's Programme for International Student Assessment (PISA) indicates that there are large disparities in the extent to which education systems equip children from different socio-economic backgrounds with foundational science knowledge and self-efficacy (Chapter 1). Girls, women, minorities, and disadvantaged youth are less likely to pursue studies or careers in science and engineering. Cultural stereotypes and a lack of role models hinder some individuals' entry into expanding fields around science, engineering, and construction fields (OECD, 2023[7]; OECD, 2023[14]). If unaddressed, these trends could suggest a compounding effect of the net-zero transition on existing inequalities, as well as segments of the population that, with the right education and training policies, could be directed towards skills and jobs required by the growing green economy (see Box 3.2).

Making connections between labour market and education policies is essential to address specific barriers and activate enabling factors for achieving the needed job market transitions. This concluding section reflects on the opportunities and challenges for education to promote the green transition via skills development and discusses a range of education policy options. It first examines how skills assessment and anticipation systems can be made effective to support evidence-based policy design. Second, it explores the role of career guidance in ensuring that individuals have the information they need to make informed study and career choices in the context of the green transition. Finally, it proposes avenues for establishing coherent skills delivery systems that offer a continuum of relevant learning opportunities throughout vocational education and training, higher education, and upskilling and re-skilling programmes.

Anticipating future skills needs for the green transition

Skills assessment and anticipation is the systematic process of predicting the future demand for specific skills in various industries or sectors (OECD, 2016[29]). It involves analysing current and emerging trends, technological advancements, economic factors, and other relevant variables to anticipate the skills that will be in high demand in the future job market. Skills forecasting directly informs career guidance initiatives, education and training policies, and workforce development strategies, to ensure that individuals are equipped with the necessary skills and competencies to meet the evolving needs of the labour market. Skills forecasting can provide initial roadmaps to respond to and prepare for changes in skill requirements brought about by a transition towards a greener economy.

In dynamic economies, the challenge lies in effectively matching the demand for skills with their supply. In an ideal scenario of a competitive labour market, prices and quantities adjust until equilibrium is achieved: firms adjust their production methods according to the available pool of skilled workers, while workers pursue training that aligns with current or anticipated economic needs. However, this model assumes perfect information —where both firms and workers have full and accurate knowledge of market conditions and future demands—a situation that hardly ever occurs. Students, workers, employers, and training institutions often lack accurate knowledge about the skills in demand over the short, medium, and long terms. This information gap can cause individuals to either underestimate or overestimate their employment prospects and can result in delays between educational or training decisions and actual labour market entry. Consequently, mismatches or shortages in skilled labour may arise (OECD, 2017[30]).

Policy makers also lack clear information on the supply of training and whether it is sufficient. In a 2016 OECD study, Labour and Education Ministries, along with social partners, such as employer organisations and trade unions, were surveyed on obstacles that hinder effective translation of skills assessment into policy. Respondents ranked 19 barriers, focusing on issues related to methodology, dissemination, and policy development. Broadly, these barriers highlight the following main challenges: coordinating stakeholders, aligning skills assessment with policymakers' needs, the lack of sufficiently disaggregated data per e.g. regions or sectors, and the difficulty in reaching consensus on skills needs and the required policy response (OECD, 2016[29]).

This sub-section examines how skills assessment and anticipation systems can be made effective to support evidence-based policy design, inform strategic decision-making, facilitate targeted education and training programmes, and foster a more agile and responsive workforce ecosystem, ultimately driving sustainable economic growth and societal resilience. It explores the importance of stakeholder involvement and the processes that can support the collection of data with adequate sectoral, geographical, and temporal resolution. It then discusses how such information can best be used to inform education policies and institutional strategies and how skills assessment and anticipation can be implemented in practice. It also addresses questions around how to balance catering to current skills needs with focusing on skills for jobs that are anticipated but have not yet materialised in the current labour market.

Ensuring stakeholder participation

Information on skills needs is most useful and effective for policymaking when there is strong co-ordination across different ministries and active stakeholder involvement (OECD, 2016[29]). Creating a comprehensive and resilient skill system to meet the challenges of the green transition requires collaboration among the diverse set of stakeholders involved in training design, provision, employment policies, and activation. Stakeholder involvement offers a valuable starting point to establish connections and communication channels among education providers, government entities, and employers, thus potentially facilitating the necessary changes for education and training systems to adapt to the evolving needs of the green transition (OECD, 2024[3]).

Different stakeholders will have different roles. For example, governments and policymakers play a crucial role in commissioning skills forecasting studies, setting policy priorities, and coordinating efforts to align skills development with sustainable development goals. As the green transition is predominantly driven by public policy, governments play a central role in setting long-term goals and ensuring compliance, necessitating proactive approaches to gather skills intelligence for evidence-based policies (OECD, 2023[31]). In addition, employers and associations in the industry sectors contribute by providing insights into current and future skills needs based on market trends, technological advancements, and regulatory changes. Finally, educational institutions, including higher education institutions, and vocational training providers utilise skills forecasting data to design curriculum and training courses tailored to the needs of sustainable/green industries.

In Norway, a 2023 report by the *Norwegian Committee for Skills Needs* offers an overview of future skill requirements in Norway, particularly addressing the challenges associated with the green transition (Kompetansebehovsutvalget, 2023[32]). The report points out gaps in collaboration between educational institutions, employers, and the government, suggesting stronger integration to ensure that training programs effectively address emerging demands. The exercise performed in the report involved various stakeholders through a structured and inclusive approach to ensure that the assessment of future skill needs was comprehensive and well-informed. The process involved social partners, including both representatives of employers and employees, expert contributions ensuring an evidence-based approach, the public sector, organisations involved in education and training as well as open dialogues to gather wide-ranging input from society at large. As a result of this multi-stakeholder approach, the committee was able to develop a comprehensive view of the skill needs and challenges faced by Norway, ensuring that its recommendations were practical, applicable, and inclusive of diverse perspectives.

Considering sectoral, regional, and temporal dimensions

OECD economies and regions vary significantly in their economic structures, workforce compositions, and environmental challenges, necessitating fine-grained, context-specific skills assessment and anticipation strategies. The development and implementation of skills assessment and anticipation practices within countries/economies requires therefore the consideration of sector-specific, regional/local dimensions as well as potentially different temporal scales.

National-level data is essential for monitoring labour-market trends and designing overarching training policies. However, it often lacks the granularity needed to identify regional and local disparities, as well as sector-specific job distributions and shortages. To address these gaps, more detailed, localised data is required to ensure that policies are responsive to the unique needs of different regions and industries. Indeed, two-thirds of Labour and Education Ministries consider that in general results from skills assessment and anticipation exercises are not sufficiently disaggregated for use at the regional, local or sectoral levels (OECD, 2016[29]).

In 2023, the European Centre for the Development of Vocational Training produced a series of skill forecast country reports providing an overview of future job and skill trends for individual EU Member States (Cedefop, n.d.[33]). The latest forecast, covering up to 2035, incorporates recent global economic trends and reflects adjustments for the European Green Deal. A common methodology and harmonised data ensure comparability across Member States, and the forecasts align with official EU economic and population projections of the economy, covering national employment projections for all sectors and industries, occupational groups, and education levels, as well as demographic changes in the working-age population. While regional disaggregation is lacking, these reports provide a solid foundation for further regional analysis.

For example, in France, Regional Observatories for Employment and Training (*Observatoire Régional Emploi Formation, OREF*) collect and analyse employment and training data at the regional level, including studies on green jobs and skills needs. For instance, the OREF for Provence, Alpes, and Côte d'Azur examined the number, gender, and qualifications of employees in green professions. Additionally, the ECECLI (*Evolution Compétences Emplois Climat Ile-de-France*) project in Ile-de-France anticipates skills needs related to the ecological and energy transition, analysing the evolution of skills in 35 professions, including new roles like ecologists and existing ones like bus drivers, who will need to adopt eco-driving techniques (OECD, 2024[3]).

Involving regional and local governments in the structure of skills assessments and anticipation exercises is especially important. Local skills systems are struggling to keep pace with the rapid change of jobs and skills needs, and to reach those who most urgently need training. Identifying both potential vulnerabilities and opportunities, through skills assessments and anticipation and responding early, can be crucial for preventing protracted regional decline, or capturing the benefits of the transition. Tailoring action to the regional context requires tripartite dialogue involving workers, employers, and public local actors including education providers, along with targeted measures to address the uneven risk of job losses across regions (OECD, 2023[5]).

Applying skills assessment and anticipation to the green transition

Recent analysis reveals that while there is growing recognition of the importance of skills assessment and anticipation methods, their application to the green transition remains relatively new and is not yet closely aligned with specific environmental targets, such as decarbonisation or circular economy goals (OECD, 2023[31]). Considering such targets and the impact of environmental policies on jobs facilitates effective long-term planning in the context of an evolving job market. It is therefore crucial to incorporate the impact of the green transition into regular skills assessment and anticipation exercises and occupational classifications, rather than examining it separately. This process involves anticipating future demands for crucial green skills amidst uncertainties such as governmental changes, technological disruptions, evolving environmental regulations and emerging technologies. It helps to foster resilience against unexpected shifts in market demands imposed by the green transition and to ensure that individuals are equipped with the necessary competencies to thrive under changing circumstances.

Moreover, the use of big data in these assessments is still limited, which affects the depth and timeliness of the results. Current approaches often prioritise general employment projections over specific skills needed for the green transition. While crucial, if specific skills are not considered, employment projections are less effective for designing policies aimed at transitioning workers and enhancing training systems (OECD, 2023[31]). Skills assessment and anticipation analysis and the integration of their outcomes into policy making would establish a direct connection between employment and training policies (OECD, 2024[3]). In Greece, the Ministry of Labour and Social Security has established the Labour Market Diagnosis Mechanism, a tool that leverages big data to identify and analyse emerging skills, including those related to the green transition. This analysis uses the ESCO skill taxonomy, alongside employment and earnings data, and is validated through quantitative business surveys and qualitative foresight panels. The top green specific skills are identified across key sectors, and the findings are used by the Ministry to effectively inform policymaking (OECD, 2024[3]).

Aligning skills assessments and anticipation with policy making needs

The challenges associated with skills assessment and anticipation exercises, such as the lack of alignment between how skills are defined and their relevance for policy decisions, the absence of sectoral and regional detail, and the insufficient involvement of stakeholders, significantly hinder the effective use of skills assessment and anticipation results in policymaking. Without sufficient detail or consensus among key actors, the findings are often too technical or broad, making it difficult for policymakers to translate the results into actionable strategies. This limits the overall impact of skills assessment and anticipation exercises on developing targeted and responsive skills policies.

Figure 3.2. Improving the evidence base through skills assessments and anticipation

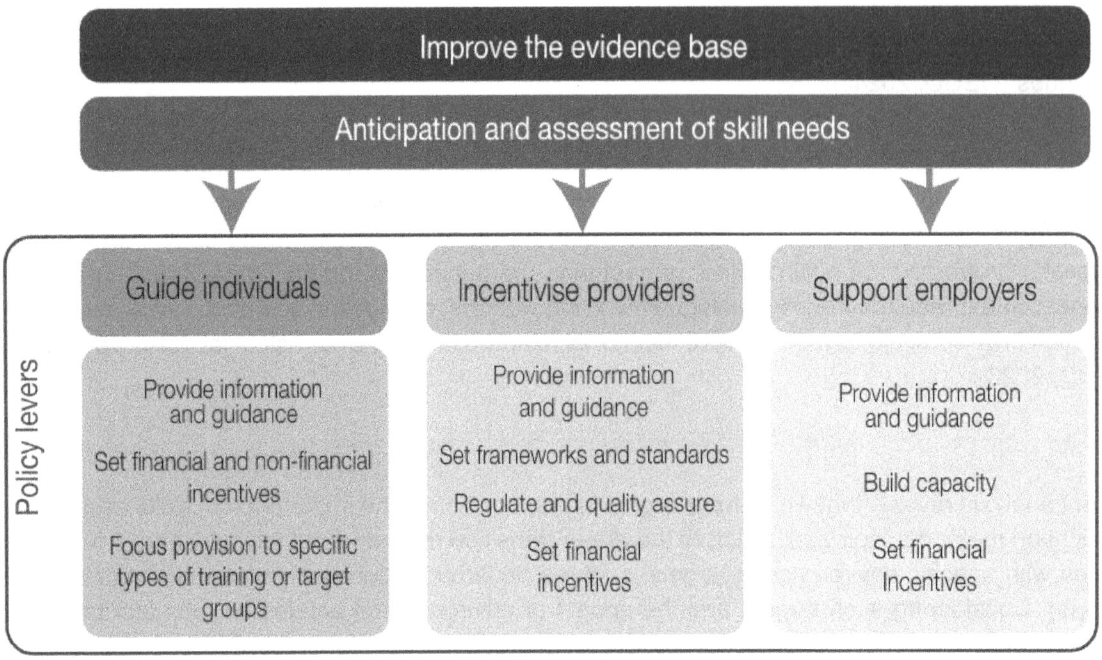

Source: (OECD, 2019[34]) *Getting Skills Right: Creating responsive adult learning systems*, https://www.oecd.org/content/dam/oecd/en/topics/policy-sub-issues/adult-learning/adult-learning-systems-2019.pdf (accessed on 2 July 2024).

Figure 3.2 outlines a framework detailing some ways in which skills assessment and anticipation exercises and frameworks can be improved to align with the needs of policymaking, by supporting different stakeholders to enhance the adaptability of adult learning systems in response to evolving skill demands (OECD, 2019[34]). Although not conceptualised specifically for the green transition, it provides numerous insights also for transformations leading to more sustainable futures:

- **Improving the evidence base**: The foundation for addressing skill imbalances starts with generating accurate data on labour market skill needs and the skills workers possess. Effective interventions depend on robust data that is accessible to stakeholders with diverse needs and interests.
- **Guiding individuals**: Existing data on skill requirements often fails to reach individuals, hindering their ability to make informed decisions about training investments and career paths. Implementing methods which direct individuals toward in-demand skills and overcome barriers to accessing relevant training emerges as crucial.
- **Incentivising providers**: Educational institutions, whether public, private, or third-sector, may lag in updating curricula to match labour-market demands. Designing financial incentives and regulations that accommodate these differences is crucial.
- **Supporting employers**: Many employers, especially small and medium-sized enterprises (SMEs), struggle to strategically assess and meet future skill requirements due to limited human resource

capacity. Supporting these employers in identifying and addressing their skill needs is vital for aligning training provision with labour-market demands.

Table 3.1 provides a comprehensive list of actions essential for implementing effective skills assessments and anticipation systems. These actions include improving data collection and sharing practices to gather detailed, sector-specific insights into skill needs and ensuring accessible dissemination of this information. Emphasis should be placed on involving stakeholders during the design phase to align skills assessments and anticipation outputs with practical requirements, fostering collaboration among educational institutions, employers, and policymakers. Prioritising sector-specific analysis and using comprehensive information systems are recommended to keep these efforts relevant and up to date. Integrating quantitative labour-market analysis with qualitative insights from industry surveys can enrich skills assessments and anticipation exercises, capturing both current demands and future trends. Additionally, building capacity for skills assessments and anticipation practitioners, integrating policies, and conducting ongoing monitoring and evaluation are crucial for maintaining the robustness and adaptability of these systems, ensuring they effectively inform education, training, and labour-market policies.

Table 3.1. Potential actions supporting the implementation of effective skills assessments and anticipation systems

Actions	Actions
Improve the governance of skill anticipation	• **Setting up a dedicated coordinating bodies**: this helps streamline skill assessment processes across various levels (national, regional, sectoral) of green industries by harmonising methodologies and sharing tools. • **Establishing independent and reputable organisations/initiatives**: creating independent bodies to conduct rigorous research and strategic planning tailored to existing and emerging green industries enhances the credibility and effectiveness in skill assessment. • **Legal obligation for stakeholder involvement**: Ensuring stakeholder (e.g. representatives from employers in green industries and trade unions, education providers) involvement through a legal mandate in skills anticipation largely enhances co-ordination.
Enhance the evidence base	• **Sharing collected data in a user-friendly** manner enhances its impact and utility for stakeholders, such as policymakers, training providers, and industry leaders in green technology sectors. • **Involving end users during the design phase** ensures the relevance and usability of skill anticipation outputs particularly for industries transitioning to green technologies. • **Prioritising specific sectors or regions** for detailed data collection to manage resource constraints effectively, such as focusing on regions or sectors with high potential for transformation. • **Combining quantitative data with qualitative insights** enriches skill anticipation efforts, offering a broader understanding of labour-market dynamics, especially in sectors undergoing rapid green transformation.

Source: Adapted from (OECD, 2019[34]) Getting Skills Right: Creating responsive adult learning systems, https://www.oecd.org/content/dam/oecd/en/topics/policy-sub-issues/adult-learning/adult-learning-systems-2019.pdf (accessed on 2 July 2024).

Efforts should be made to ensure that skills assessments and anticipation processes are inclusive and equitable, considering the diverse needs and backgrounds of individuals in accessing green job opportunities. This involves addressing various dimensions to ensure fair and inclusive access to skills assessments and anticipation dialogues, which must bring together multiple stakeholders, including underrepresented groups, minority communities, and disadvantaged populations. This can be achieved through targeted outreach, engagement initiatives, and consultation forums that solicit input and perspectives from these groups (OECD, 2019[34]). By embracing inclusivity and equity in skills forecasting, societies can leverage the full talent pool, enhance social cohesion, and promote sustainable economic growth that benefits all individuals and communities. This marks also an opportunity for course-correction to ensure that the future workforce is more inclusive, gender-balanced, and enabling of equal opportunity across different transitioning sectors of the economy (IEA, 2022[35]).

Enhancing career guidance to support pathways into sustainable careers

Globally, skills gaps and shortages are increasingly acknowledged as critical obstacles constraining progress towards the green transition (Keese and Marcolin, 2023[36]). This is despite the fact that many of the skills necessary to carry out green-related jobs already exist in the labour market (OECD, 2024[3]). Career guidance systems can serve as bridges connecting the interests and skills of people with labour-market demand, facilitating effective communication between both sides. However, results from the OECD's Programme for International Student Assessment (PISA) 2022 show that 15-year-old student participation in key guidance activities remains limited in many OECD countries (OECD, 2023[37]) and need to be enhanced. A survey conducted in six countries (Chile, France, Germany, Italy, New Zealand and the United States) showed that there is significant demand for career guidance among adults, with 43% of adults having consulted a career guidance advisor in the past five years, and most engaging in multiple interactions with advisors (OECD, 2021[38]).

This section explores the role of career guidance in support of an inclusive and fair green transition. It examines how career guidance systems at the school level and beyond can best make green guidance an integral part of general career guidance and examine the role of effective career guidance systems in addressing social inequality, ensuring a just transition. Given that access to career guidance is strongly patterned by the demographic characteristics of learners, it considers how career guidance interventions can address inequities in who benefits from the green transition. In addition, beyond the school level, it explores how lifelong learning systems can be strengthened via effective career guidance systems to help people navigate changing labour-market demands in line with the green transition and make decisions for re-skilling and upskilling at different stages of their careers.

Guiding individuals into sustainable and resilient careers

The complexity of the labour-market changes discussed above complicates advising students and adults on opportunities related to the green transition (Chang and Mann, 2024[39]). This complexity arises because many skills do not clearly fall into the categories of green or polluting occupations, but rather exist along a spectrum depending on how they are applied within the different industries. As a result, providing clear and simple guidance on skills needed to benefit from green job opportunities becomes challenging, making it difficult for individuals to navigate and capitalise on the green transition.

However, Chang and Mann (2024[39]) find that, despite the complexities of aligning education and career guidance with labour-market demands, young people show a strong interest in participating in the fight against climate change. Surveys from around the world indicate a significant commitment among youth to pursue green jobs and contribute to sustainability efforts. Career guidance can nurture this commitment, emphasising the potential implications of their chosen education paths in terms of climate action, and enabling them to build a foundation for a career in the new and evolving green-driven occupations (OECD, 2024[3]).

For adults, career guidance is a crucial policy tool that helps them to successfully navigate the ever-changing labour market by providing advice and information on job and training opportunities. Career guidance is a valuable way to facilitate skill matching between workers and jobs, guiding workers towards jobs that fit their skill profile well. Skill mismatches can result in lower earnings and job satisfaction, higher risk of job loss, loss of competitiveness, and lower economic growth. Persistent mismatches entail large costs for individuals, employers, and society, and could slow down the transition to net zero (OECD, 2024[3]). Well-designed career guidance can limit the incidence of such mismatches.

However, relatively low uptake of career guidance remains an issue. In particular, groups already facing disadvantage in the labour market tend to use career guidance services less than the population at large (OECD, 2024[3]). The majority of adults who do not participate in training (82%) report that no available training options appealed to them, indicating a lack of awareness about the importance of training in the current labour market, challenges in finding appropriate guidance opportunities and/or inadequacies of the educational offer (OECD, 2021[38]). This highlights the need to develop labour-market aligned education and training options as well as relevant and accessible study and career guidance.

A range of actors are involved in the provision of career guidance. Traditionally, the public employment service (PES) is the most used career guidance provider. Several countries are undertaking actions to strengthen the provision of career guidance relating to the net-zero transition within the PES. However, education and training institutions, employers, private career guidance providers, and dedicated public guidance agencies each have important roles in providing career guidance. Co-ordination between these actors can ensure the effective and efficient provision of career guidance. For instance, public-private collaborations are necessary to inform both the content of guidance and its use by adults (OECD, 2024[3]).

In an OECD policy questionnaire (OECD, 2023[40]), only nine out of twenty-six respondent OECD countries reported having career guidance initiatives in place to facilitate workers' transitions into green jobs. This indicates strong potential to enhance targeted career guidance programmes. In some cases, countries report having added an environmental angle to existing, broader guidance programmes. In other cases, career guidance has been added as a component of a wider environmental training programme.

In the context of the green transition, green career guidance (or 'green guidance') should not be seen as a specialised or optional aspect of general career guidance, but rather as an integral component of it. Given the urgency of climate change and other environmental challenges, as well as the risks of skills shortages for the green transition, it is essential that education systems fully incorporate green guidance into standard career counselling practices, ensuring it receives the attention it deserves (Chang and Mann, 2024[39]).

Irving and Liévano (2019[41]) argue that the disconnect between educational and career guidance on the one hand, and the principles of social and environmental justice on the other have rarely been effectively bridged. The authors contend that there is significant potential to expand guidance and education to include transformative dialogues, offering opportunities to envision positive futures in the context of climate and other environmental challenges and highlighting connections between educational pathways and broader social and environmental goals. This underscores the importance of offering young people and adults a diverse array of perspectives, enabling them to critique, examine, and explore the concept of "meaningful career".

Building on previous discussions in this report, green guidance should extend beyond merely equipping youth and adults with advice on technical skills, knowledge, and competencies needed to meet employer needs and economic demands. Indeed, green guidance can also empower individuals to develop systems thinking and critical thinking skills, fostering agency to make career choices that align with sustainable futures. This approach not only promotes safer and more resilient career paths but also ensures their longevity in a rapidly changing world.

Carosin and Canzittu (2019[42]) set out a framework aiming at identifying and developing career guidance systems that are relevant to the complex 21st century challenges faced by current and future generations. Through career guidance, this framework aims at empowering individuals to transform their capacity to act into the power to pursue careers that foster a collective consciousness of global challenges, particularly the environmental issues confronting societies today. Figure 3.3 illustrates this framework, which conceptualises career guidance as a learning experience in its own right.

Figure 3.3. Learning experience through career guidance

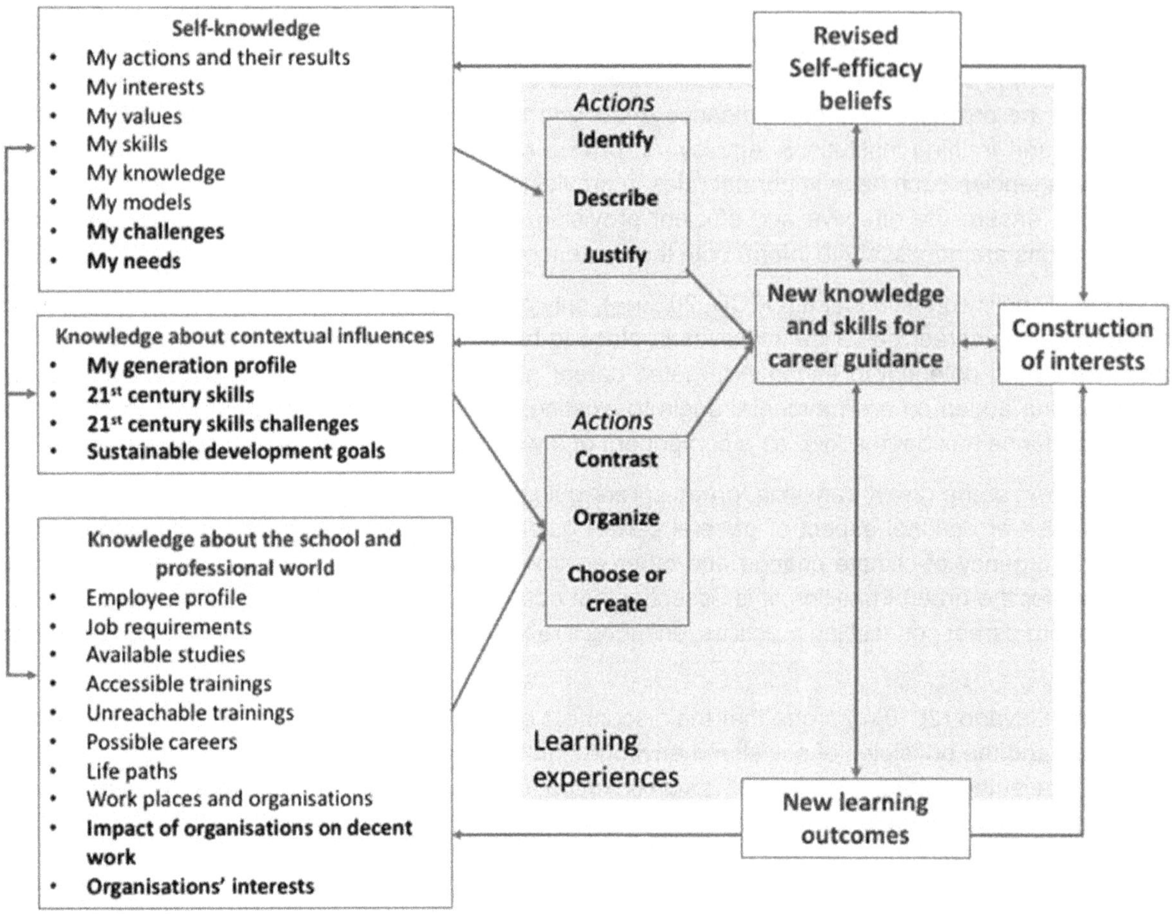

Source: (Carosin and Canzittu, 2019[42]) "A reflection on career guidance skills for the 21st century in a Guidance Oriented Approach to Learning (GOAL)", Vol. 8, pp. 375-391, https://doi.org/10.34862/sp.2019.8.

The authors identify three sets of pedagogical tools to foster career guidance systems that are relevant for the 21st century. The first set of pedagogical tools focuses on self-awareness, helping individuals identify and understand their personal characteristics, such as interests, values, and skills, and how these can inform their career choices. The second set emphasises societal context, encouraging individuals to contrast and critically evaluate available knowledge about the labour market, sustainable development, and the impact of various industries, thereby fostering critical thinking. The third set addresses self-knowledge through the lens of the learners' generation, guiding individuals to reflect on their profiles, values, and aspirations, and facilitating discussions that connect their personal development with societal roles and future career paths (Carosin and Canzittu, 2019[42]).

Importantly, this framework takes a holistic approach to situating career guidance within a global context, encompassing the broad range of challenges facing societies today, without singling out the climate and environmental problems. Considering that that many challenges facing societies today are intertwined and that solutions do not exist in isolated parts of the system, but rather rely on a systemic approach to the multi-faceted crises, it provides a valuable reflection and potential way forward for more effective career guidance systems.

Figure 3.4. A model of green guidance

Conceptual model drawing upon current green guidance practices and OECD analysis of longitudinal datasets that explores the relationships between teenage career development and better employment outcomes in adulthood.

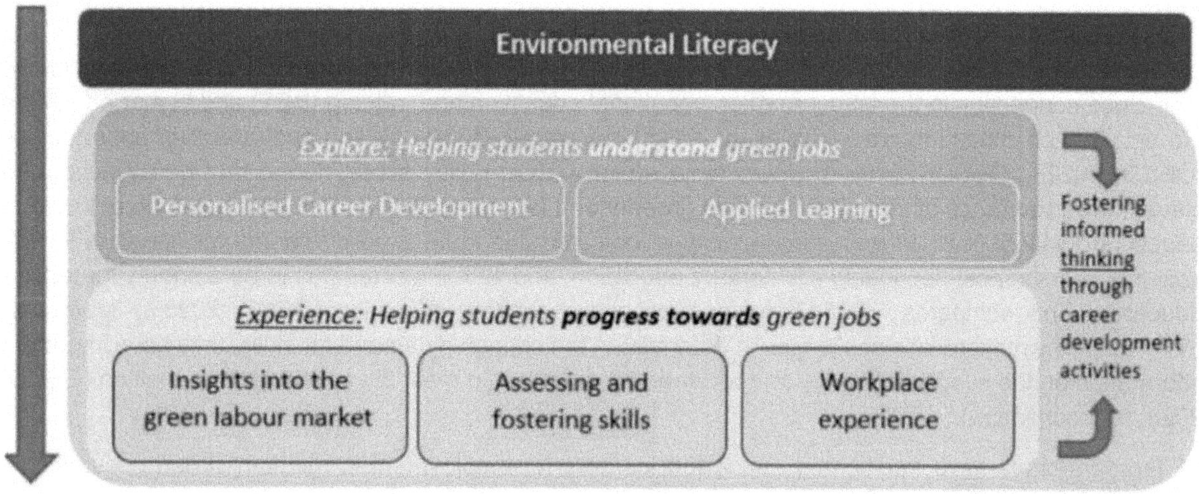

Source: (OECD, 2024[43]) Cultivating green futures: Helping students understand and progress towards green jobs", *OECD Education Policy Perspectives*, No. 104, OECD Publishing, Paris, https://doi.org/10.1787/7c9912c5-en.

Aligned with these findings, the OECD Career Readiness framework for green guidance (Figure 3.4) proposes a conceptual model that emphasizes the importance of building upon and strengthening foundational environmental literacy. This approach empowers students from an early age to connect their classroom learning with future career possibilities. Furthermore, green guidance should provide students with opportunities to explore various occupational fields in greater depth through authentic, first-hand interactions with professionals in relevant sectors and visits to their workplaces. By doing so, students are better equipped to navigate their educational and training journeys, linking their daily learning efforts with envisioned future careers (OECD, 2024[43]), thereby transforming career guidance itself into a meaningful learning experience.

Career guidance, social inequality, and social mobility

Access to career development is heavily influenced by socio-economic background, gender, and ethnicity, leading to significant inequalities in employment outcomes and career aspirations (OECD, 2024[44]). Evidence from a number of career guidance programmes from across the world reveals that there are four thematic areas through which guidance systems can address barriers to labour-market progression. These include: (i) providing intensified support for disadvantaged groups, (ii) enhancing the professional capacity of guidance practitioners to address inequalities, (iii) building social capital by connecting students with professionals in their desired fields, and (iv) encouraging a critical understanding of personal relationships with the labour market to empower informed career decisions (OECD, 2024[44]). By integrating these strategies with a focus on the green transition, career guidance can also steer students towards emerging green jobs, ensuring that the benefits of a sustainable economy are accessible to all, regardless of background.

Career guidance also has the potential to address social inequality ensuring a more just transition. There are two main ways in which career guidance can achieve this objective. First, career guidance systems need to be made equally accessible to students from different socio-economic backgrounds and across various segments of the labour market, from high-skilled to low-skilled workers. Second, by taking a holistic approach, career guidance can guide individuals towards professions where they can actively work to reduce disparities and promote sustainability. This approach ensures that career advice is not merely about individual success, but also about making a positive impact on the broader community.

Building a coherent skills delivery landscape for the green transition

The structural changes to our economies and societies brought on by the transition to net zero require that the current and future workforce develop the right skills to prepare for and adapt to these changes. Given their close connection to the labour market, vocational education and training (VET) and higher education are uniquely positioned to provide relevant initial programmes and re-skilling and upskilling opportunities (OECD, 2022[1]; OECD, 2023[45]). However, a recent OECD policy survey found that policy actions to elevate the importance of education towards greener and fairer societies primarily focus on lower levels of education. Only 50% of 34 education ministries indicated this to be a policy priority for attention for the next five years in post-secondary non-tertiary education, and 42% indicated this to be a priority for tertiary education. This compares with 64% for primary and secondary education (OECD, 2023[7]). Moreover, much as policy makers face challenges in determining the changing demand for skills, they have imperfect information on the supply of training and whether it is sufficient to meet the needs of the transition (OECD, 2024, forthcoming[28]).

VET programmes have traditionally supported learners for employment in medium-skilled occupations, some of which are at a risk of displacement due to the green transition (OECD, 2023[5]). At the same time, many green jobs are highly technical in nature, putting VET -at various levels- at the heart of the green transition. Throughout the section, the analysis highlights three complementary approaches that can help adapt VET provision to the context of the green transition.

- First, adapting initial VET programmes at upper-secondary, post-secondary and tertiary levels to prepare labour market entrants for new and emerging occupations and occupations that content is changing in a rapidly greening economy.
- Second, creating new and more flexible opportunities for the workforce to upskill and reskill by adapting continuing VET provision.
- Third, improving opportunities and pathways for VET learners to progress to higher levels of education and training, as evidence shows that high-skilled and educated workers have predominantly captured the employment opportunities brought on by the green transition (OECD, 2023[5]).

Higher education institutions (HEIs) also need to accelerate the alignment of their existing programmes and curricula to the skills required by a greening labour market. As core suppliers of advanced knowledge and skills to economies and societies, adding a green lens to their programme offerings will be crucial to cultivating workers that can spearhead the much-needed innovations to accelerate the transition to net zero (Kato, Galán-Muros and Weko, 2020[46]; OECD, 2024[47]). While HEIs traditionally focus on the provision of post-secondary education to young adults, external factors such as rapidly ageing populations and public funding pressures are pushing the sector to create more flexible and tailored upskilling and re-skilling offerings for adult learners at different stages of their careers (OECD, 2023[48]; OECD, 2024[49]).

In addition, several countries have supported the creation of new and more professionally oriented HEIs, such as universities of applied science (UAS) and polytechnics (OECD, 2008[50]; OECD, 2019[51]), often in response to demands from students and employers for more applied forms of higher education and to skills-based hiring practices in companies (Gonzales Ehlinger and Stephany, 2023[52]; Ehlers and Eigbrecht, 2024[53]). In many countries, these practice-oriented providers play a key role in expanding opportunities for learners, especially VET graduates, due to the more applied nature of their courses (OECD, 2022[54]). In addition, other forms of specialised professionally-oriented programmes have developed to provide skills and training necessary for the greening economy. See for example Box 3.6 on the case of green entrepreneurship.

Box 3.4. Supporting skills needed for green entrepreneurship

Stimulating green entrepreneurship is an important lever that governments can use to drive the net-zero transition. Green entrepreneurship can help to develop and propagate new technologies and business models, create new markets and drive change in the business sector. To tap into this potential, governments often provide direct support to green entrepreneurs, for example, through training and support for incubation and acceleration programmes. These direct supports are typically situated within a broader set of policies that build demand for green solutions. Green entrepreneurship policies are initiated both by national and sub-national governments, often in partnership with private sector actors. This implies a need for a co-ordinated policy approach that enables and encourages collaboration between different actors.

Entrepreneurs leverage a wide range of skills in order to start, operate and grow their businesses. These include both the workforce skills required of employees and additional skills that reflect the demands of running a business (e.g. identifying opportunities, financial literacy). Green entrepreneurs may also require additional skills related to adapting products, services, and processes to be supportive of climate action goals and related environmental requirements and regulations. Training and education programmes that combine these different elements can be valuable in providing would-be green entrepreneurs with the skills needed to drive green and innovative business. While some small-scale training programmes have been implemented, skills gaps remain an issue in many OECD countries, and supporting training for green entrepreneurs should therefore be a priority area for future policy development.

An increasingly common approach to supporting the development of green skills among entrepreneurs is through dedicated incubation and acceleration programmes for green businesses. These programmes typically provide a combination of training, individualised coaching and advisory services, access to networks, investors or markets, a workspace, and shared facilities and equipment. They can be a valuable way of nurturing early-stage start-ups and accelerating the growth of more established businesses. While the number of specialised incubation and acceleration programmes has been increasing in recent years, continued government support is needed to fund and build the capacity of such programmes.

Source: (OECD, 2022[55]) *Policies to Support Green Entrepreneurship: Building a Hub for Green Entrepreneurship in Denmark*, OECD Studies on SMEs and Entrepreneurship, OECD Publishing, Paris, https://doi.org/10.1787/e92b1946-en.

To achieve the triple objective of aligning provision with the competencies needed by a greening economy, expanding upskilling and re-skilling opportunities, and improving transitions and pathways for learners across VET and higher education, both sectors must find ways to "better integrate the world of learning with the world of work" across education, training, upskilling and re-skilling strategies (OECD, 2022, p. 6[56]).

In this context, education providers must strengthen co-operation, not just with each other, but also with greening industries, local governments and other relevant actors to align their provision with regional skills needs and national priorities. For example, a VET provider offering training for construction workers and a university educating structural engineers, might engage with the same construction companies to identify relevant skills needs and jointly organise work-based learning, thereby preparing graduates from both sectors for future work together. In practice, however, such collaboration across VET providers, HEIs and employers may prove challenging, as it is often impeded by culture clashes, inner/outsider dynamics and vertical hierarchies, which may hinder effective collaboration (OECD, 2023[57]; Staring and Butler, forthcoming[58]).

In addition to this, several countries face challenges in aligning national priorities with those of regional or local authorities and stakeholders. Local governments are well-placed to act as initiators of local skills coalitions that improve the design and delivery of local policies and secure public buy-in for the green transition (OECD, 2023[5]). However, actions focused on joining local employment and skills policies may clash with an overarching and more long-term vision for skills development at system level. This is where central government leadership and steering can help facilitate co-operation around a common green skills agenda (Dowling, 2015[59]; European Commission, 2018[60]).

In recent years, some OECD jurisdictions have embarked on "a national effort to create an accessible and organised tertiary system" (Teo et al., 2023, p. viii[20]). This is especially the case in countries where VET is primarily offered from age 16 onwards (for example, in Canada, the United States, Ireland), with VET modules being introduced on a modular basis in general upper-secondary programmes. In these countries, VET and higher education are strategically positioned as being part of a single "skills delivery landscape" (Withers, 2023[61]), with the common objective of supporting skills development centred on key societal challenges.

Building on a recent mapping of policies to strengthen synergies across the VET and higher education sectors by Staring and Butler (forthcoming[58]) (see also Figure 3.5), the following sections discuss a set of strategies through which governments may support the development of more flexible and coherent post-secondary education and training system:1) building a strategic vision for skills development; 2) adapting qualifications and curricula; 3) removing barriers to participation in re-skilling and upskilling; 4) supporting VET and higher education providers in enhancing the lifelong learning offer; and 5) strengthening professional learning of teaching staff.

Figure 3.5. Strategies for building an inclusive skills delivery landscape for the green transition

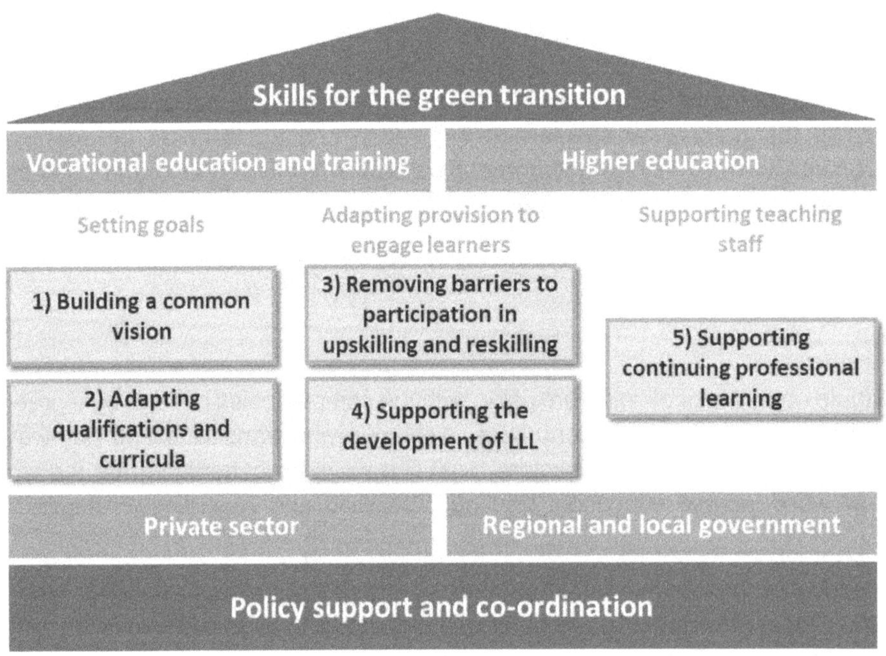

Source: Adapted from the "Future Skills in Higher Education" model developed by Ehlers and Eigbrecht (eds.) (2024[53]), *Creating the University of the Future: A Global View on Future Skills and Future Higher Education*, Zukunft der Hochschulbildung [Future Higher Education], Karlsruhe, pp. xiv, https://link.springer.com/book/10.1007/978-3-658-42948-5.

Building a strategic vision for skills development across VET and higher education

In recent years, some OECD jurisdictions have carried out comprehensive reviews of their post-secondary VET, higher education, research and skills systems with a view to developing cross-sectoral strategies and creating overarching bodies to implement skills policies spanning both sectors (Staring and Butler, forthcoming[62]). In many cases, this has included a focus on skills development for the green transition and improving pathways and transitions across VET and higher education. In some cases, strategic performance agreements are used as a tool to incentivise providers to align with national priorities such as environmental sustainability, especially in the higher education sector. In some cases, part of an institution's core funding is tied to the implementation of such agreements (Jongbloed et al., 2022[63]).

To give some examples, Ireland, Norway, Scotland (UK), Singapore and Wales (UK) have recently embarked on strategies to strengthen tertiary alignment around a common skills agenda (Staring and Butler, forthcoming[62]). In Scotland (UK), for example, the Further and Higher Education Funding Council (SFC) undertook a national review of its VET, higher education and research systems (SFC, 2021[64]). Based on the findings of this review, four strategic objectives and twenty priorities were identified to guide skills development across the three sectors from 2022 to 2027 (SFC, 2022[65]). Climate change is a key theme underpinning all priorities and described as "a collective responsibility" for all sectors. Box 3.5 provides more detailed examples from Australia and Ireland.

Box 3.5. Building a coherent landscape for skills development across the VET and higher education sectors in Australia and Ireland

The Australian Tertiary Education Commission

In November 2022, Australia's Department of Education appointed the Universities Accord Panel to carry out an independent review of the higher education sector to meet current and future skills needs. In February 2024, the Panel's report was published, including a National Tertiary Objective, accompanied by 47 recommendations, to drive "stronger alignment between VET and higher education, in pursuit of a stronger skills system". The National Tertiary Objective includes a specific focus on "driving] national economic and social development and environmental sustainability" (Australian Department of Education, 2024, p. 16[66]).

In response to the Panel's recommendations, in July 2024 the Department of Education started the process of establishing an Australian Tertiary Education Commission (ATEC), which would include representatives from the main regulatory bodies for Australia's skills, VET, employment and higher education sectors. The government envisages that ATEC will need to play a leading role in identifying skills needs (in co-operation with bodies such as Jobs and Skills Australia) and, based on this, facilitate purposeful collaboration between all government departments, tertiary education providers, industry, employers, communities and unions to develop a high-quality, engaging and transformative.

Ireland's Department for Further Education, Higher Education, Research and Skills

In 2020, Ireland established the Department of Further and Higher Education, Research, Innovation and Science (DFHERIS) to progress a unified tertiary system. DFHERIS does this by, among others, fostering strategic alignment between the actions of the Further Education and Skills Service (SOLAS) and Higher Education Authority (HEA), which are responsible for the resourcing and policy development of Ireland's further (i.e. VET) and higher education sectors.

A concrete example of alignment between further and higher education facilitated by DFHERIS can be found in the national priorities underpinning the strategic performance agreements between SOLAS, the HEA and providers. The agreements between SOLAS and the 16 Education and Training Boards (ETBs) in Ireland—who manage more than 200 VET providers—now include specific targets related to embedding core green skills modules in VET programmes. Likewise, the performance agreements between all Irish HEIs and the HEA include performance objectives related to institutions' contribution to climate, environment and sustainability across four pillars of institutional activity: a) teaching and learning, b) research and innovation, c) engagement, and d) promoting access and participation.

Source: Based on SOLAS (2022[67]), Transforming Learning Strategic Performance Agreements: The Further Education & Training System 2022-2024, Further Education and Skills Service (SOLAS), Dublin, https://www.solas.ie/f/70398/x/807fb6e096/fet-system-report.pdf (accessed on 6 December 2024) and (HEA, 2023[68]), Strategic Performance Framework 2023-2028, Higher Education Authority (HEA), Dublin, https://hea.ie/assets/uploads/2017/04/System_Performance_Framework_2023-2028.pdf. (accessed on 6 December 2024)

Adapting qualifications and curricula to changing labour market needs

Beyond a national vision for delivery, objectives for skills development for the green transition need to be reflected in qualification and curriculum frameworks. In all OECD systems, the structure, content, teaching and outcomes of VET and higher education programmes are guided by national regulation and subject- or profession-specific curriculum frameworks. These frameworks often follow international standards [e.g. the European Qualifications Framework for lifelong learning for EU member states (Council of the EU, 2009[69])] and seek to establish common standards and comparability in student learning outcomes, regardless of the type of institution or programme they graduate from. They also seek to promote transitions between different types of programmes and institutions, lifelong learning, and international mobility of learners and workers (OECD, 2022[70]; OECD, 2024[47]).

Within these broad curriculum frameworks, VET and higher education providers have varying degrees of autonomy in curriculum design. Giving education providers sufficient autonomy for curriculum design is generally regarded as crucial to ensure responsiveness to emerging skills needs—such as those required by the green transition. Depending on the level of education, the types of institutions and programmes and the education system's overall maturity, providers will enjoy greater or less flexibility to adapt national standards to their local context, for example to integrate content or subjects tailored to the specific needs or interests of the learners or regions they serve. Lower levels of education, VET providers and practice-oriented HEIs will typically be subject to more detailed requirements than universities offering programmes that have less of a direct link to specific professions (OECD, 2022[70]; Staring and Butler, forthcoming[58]).

Regardless of providers' level of autonomy for programme design, curriculum developers face the common challenge of knowing: a) which competencies to prioritise, and b) where best to integrate these competencies in often already overloaded curricula (see Chapter 1). Adding content related to the green transition requires choosing between adapting existing courses (which requires finding a link to existing content), creating additional formal courses, or expanding work-based learning (which may require the omission of other courses) (OECD, 2023[57]; OECD, 2024[47]). Another challenge relates to the time lag and costs associated with conventional approaches to mapping skills needs and updating curricula (OECD, 2020[71]; Eckel, 2023[72]).

To accelerate curriculum adaptation processes in VET and higher education, several governments foster collaboration between industry, education and training providers to map sector needs, identify current and future skills demands and, based on this, develop guidance and frameworks to support curriculum adaptation by providers. Such frameworks either seek to offer an overview of skills in support of the green transition common across different subjects, or on skills specific to certain disciplines or occupations which are believed to play a key role in advancing the green transition (see Box 3.6 for examples from Austria and Singapore).

Box 3.6. National support for curriculum updates in Austria and Singapore

Supporting curriculum adaptation of VET providers and vocational colleges in Austria

In 2020, the European Commission (EC) published the "Osnabrück Declaration on vocational education and training for transition to digital and green economies" (EC, 2020[73]). The Declaration includes four broad objectives, one of which is to promote sustainability in VET. In response to this Declaration, Austria developed a National Implementation Plan, including thirty actions to support the VET sector with the adaptation to green skills (BMBWF, 2022[74]). One of these (Action 13) includes a curriculum reform for intermediate VET providers (*Berufsbildende mittlere Schulen – BMS*), which offer ISCED (International Standard Classification of Education) level 3 and 4 programmes, and vocational colleges (*Berufsbildende höhere Schulen – BHS*) offering short-cycle tertiary programmes at ISCED level 5. This is done through two studies: one to support those involved in developing curricula in including "transversal" green skills, and one to support a specific focus on developing prototypical competence descriptions for construction technology.

Skills Frameworks to promote skills mastery and lifelong learning for the Singapore workforce

In 2021, Singapore's Ministry of Education established SkillsFuture Singapore (SFS) as a government agency with dedicated responsibility to support universities, polytechnics and institutes of technical education (ITEs) in developing multiple pathways for skills acquisition and mastery. One of the key objectives of SKS is to promote a "shift away from an education system that relies on front-loading within the first 2 decades of an individual's life, towards continuing education and learning over a lifetime" (Singapore Ministry of Education, 2023, p. xiv[75]).

To support VET and higher education providers with the development of new and industry-relevant qualifications, SFS has developed 35 Skills Frameworks to support the implementation of Industry Transformation Maps. This includes specific skills frameworks for the Energy & Power sectors, Environmental Services and Landscape as sectors that will play a key role in achieving the transition to net zero. Each Skills Framework includes: a) sector information (i.e. key trends and workforce profiles in a given sector); b) a skills map (i.e. an overview of the main job roles, critical work functions, key tasks, skills and competencies needed by that industry); and c) a list of skills and competencies under two broad categories: technical skills and competencies, and critical core skills (SFS, 2024[76]).

Source: (Singapore Ministry of Education, 2023, p. xiv[75]) Education Statistics Digest 2023, Singapore Ministry of Education, https://www.moe.gov.sg/-/media/files/about-us/education-statistics-digest-2023.pdf (accessed on 18 July 2024); (SFS, 2024[76]) Skills Frameworks to support the Industry Transformation Maps, SkillFuture Singapore (SFS), https://www.skillsfuture.gov.sg/skills-framework (accessed on 18 July 2024); (EC, 2020[73]) Osnabrück Declaration on vocational education and training as an enabler of recovery and just transitions to digital and green economies, European Commission, Brussels, https://ec.europa.eu/social/main.jsp?catId=738&langId=en&pubId=8441&furtherPubs=yes (accessed on 31 July 2024); (BMBWF, 2022[74]) Nationaler Implementierungsplan (NIP) Österreich [National Implementation Plan (NIP) Austria], Ministry of Education, Science and Training (BMBWF), Ministry of Digitalisation and Labour Market (BMDW), https://ec.europa.eu/social/BlobServlet?docId=26326&langId=en (accessed on 31 July 2024).

Removing barriers to participation in upskilling and re-skilling

As discussed throughout the chapter, upskilling and re-skilling opportunities are crucial to support workers at risk of displacement due to the green transition. According to a policy questionnaire distributed to all OECD countries, many governments have launched publicly funded training programmes to upskill and reskill workers and jobseekers for the green transition (OECD, 2024, forthcoming[28]). Yet, recent OECD analysis highlights that despite the risk of job displacement, workers in GHG-intensive occupations currently tend to train significantly less than other workers (OECD, 2024[3]). Moreover, while participation in training is low among workers in general, it appears to be especially low among highly impacted workers such as those in the most vulnerable regions and sectors (Borgonovi et al., 2023[16]). Globally, workers in GHG-intensive jobs show lower training participation rates, with especially concerning disparities in countries where training rates are already low (OECD, 2023[5]).

Ensuring equal access to education and training opportunities and addressing barriers to participation are key policy priorities. One of the main barriers to adult participation in upskilling and re-skilling by adults is lack of motivation. Other barriers include lack of time or money, lack of awareness of programmes, lack of recognition of their prior learning, inconvenient place and mode of learning, and lack of flexible provision. This sub-section will address these barriers in turn and provide policy options for addressing them.

First, a potential barrier hindering participation relates to the financial costs associated with upskilling and re-skilling. There are both direct costs to participation (such as tuition fees) as well as more indirect costs linked to the potential loss of income due to having to take shorter working hours or having to pay for additional childcare in order to free up the time needed to participate (OECD, 2024[49]). Government support can thus help workers in covering some of their costs. In some countries, adults can receive financial support or time from the government to engage in upskilling or re-skilling. The SkillsFuture Credit is a publicly funded student finance mechanism first introduced in 2015 as part of Singapore's SkillsFuture initiative (see Box 3.6 earlier in this section). All Singaporeans aged 25 or over receive a non-expirable allowance of SGD 500, which they can use to cover the costs of eligible courses listed on the MySkillsFuture portal (Government of Singapore, 2024[77]). Linking financial support to courses aimed at advancing skills development for the green transition may be an option that governments may wish to consider moving forward.

A second obstacle for adults is lack of awareness about available upskilling or re-skilling opportunities, especially among learners with lower levels of prior educational achievement (Kis and Windisch, 2018[78]; OECD, 2019[79]; OECD, 2019[80]). To overcome this challenge, some countries have invested in career guidance (see Section on Enhancing career guidance to support pathways into sustainable careers) and online information portals, providing a user-friendly overview of upskilling and re-skilling opportunities. In some countries, portals have been developed with a specific focus on the green transition. An example is Finland's Climate University, an online platform which brings together courses on climate change from 27 HEIs. An explicit priority of the network is to support upskilling and re-skilling for the green transition (Climate University, 2023[81]).

A third challenge many adults face is lack of recognition of the knowledge and skills they have already acquired through non-formal and informal learning. The long administrative processes associated with recognition of prior learning (RPL) processes can present a major barrier to participation in upskilling and re-skilling in VET and higher education. RPL can be defined as "the process by which authorised bodies validate an individual's existing knowledge and skills" (OECD, 2023, p. 13[82]). Historically, these systems were developed to recognise formal learning in the form of prior educational qualifications. More recently, however, governments have started to integrate non-formal and informal learning in their procedures, as well as changing existing credit transfer and national qualification frameworks to enhance adult learning (Tuck, 2007[83]; Auzinger, Ulicna and Messerer, 2016[84]; OECD, 2023[85]).

The improvement of RPL processes will require co-ordination across sectors (i.e. VET, higher education, and adult learning), the labour market and government (e.g. departments responsible for education and labour market policy) (OECD, 2023[48]). In France, for example, a system for recognising and validating the professional experience of adults (*Validation des acquis de l'expérience – VAE*) has been in place for more than 20 years. Through the VAE procedure, anyone with at least one year of professional experience can apply for a professional certificate which can be used to enter formal learning programmes in VET or higher education. The process requires applicants to fill out an application form in which they indicate which skills they have acquired and how, for example through volunteering, self-employment or community service (French Ministry of Education and Youth, 2024[86]).

Inconvenient mode of provision may be another obstacle to engagement. For adult learners, having flexibility in what and how to study is crucial so they can follow individualised pathways that reflect their prior experience, and allow them to combine upskilling and re-skilling with work and family duties (OECD, 2023[82]). Yet, in many countries, regulatory barriers impede VET providers and HEIs to develop more flexible study programmes (Staring and Butler, forthcoming[58]). For example, some VET providers and HEIs face restrictions to developing part-time programmes, expanding students' course choice (e.g. due to a high number of mandatory courses), or offering programmes in online, hybrid or blended formats. In addition, the nature of some green-related training, which may involve hands-on learning of new technologies, may be challenging to deliver virtually. In any case, removing legislative barriers to the development of flexible formats of provision is thus crucial.

In this context, the emergence of micro-credentials[4] has pushed several governments to introduce the regulatory changes needed to advance upskilling and re-skilling. Australia's National Micro-credentials Framework seeks to "encourage greater cohesion in the design, development and delivery of micro-credentials across both the Australian education system and broader industry" (Government of Australia, 2022, p. 4[87]). The government also offers targeted funding for micro-credentials development in areas of national importance for upskilling and re-skilling (Clare, 2023[88]). Hungary has recently introduced amendments to its Adult Education Act to make VET and higher education providers explicitly responsible for the development of more flexible upskilling and re-skilling programmes for adults. In the higher education sector specifically, it has also removed several regulatory barriers impeding HEIs to develop fully online and hybrid study programmes (Hungarian Parliament, 2023[89]; OECD, 2023[90]).

A final important barrier is related to geographical factors. As highlighted above, regions with less green labour markets, despite facing greater risks and changes due to the green transition, also record lower participation in training programmes.

To tackle the urban-rural divide (see Section on The regional dimension of labour-market changes) and support skills development in regions that are particularly affected by or well positioned to tackle climate change, some governments are investing in the development of regional dual sector programmes (Staring and Butler, forthcoming[58]). Such programmes are jointly designed and delivered by VET providers and HEIs, often in partnership with employers, and support skills development adapted to the needs of a particular region, sub-region or sector. There is a strong focus in these programmes on bottom-up, collaborative and place-based approaches between students, instructors and employers, focused on the immediate environment within which these actors function.

Such local, bottom-up organised training can be crucial for workers transitioning from high carbon-emitting to green industries (OECD, 2023[19]). In addition, they offer alternative pathways and transitions between VET and higher education, making them more attractive to learners looking for further study and work opportunities. The development of a forward-looking, comprehensive, and well-targeted adult learning system can become a regional advantage, attracting innovative investments, and allowing restructuring of local economies facing high risks due to the transition (OECD, 2023[5]). Box 3.7 provides examples from France, the Netherlands and Scotland (UK). In Europe, the European Commission's Pact for Skills and

Centres of Vocational Excellence programmes play a key role in fostering such partnerships, including around climate change (EC, 2024[91]).

Box 3.7. Supporting regional and sectoral lifelong learning ecosystems in France, the Netherlands and Scotland (UK)

Professional Campus and Excellence Qualifications in France

Campus des métiers et des qualifications (Professional Campus and Excellence Qualifications) was created in 2013 with the aim of aligning education and vocational training with the economic needs of different regions in France. These campuses focus on developing skills in sectors critical to national and regional growth, such as aeronautics, energy, and digital industries. The governance of the Professional Campus is decentralised and collaborative, involving a partnership between regional presidents and academic rectors. These authorities are responsible for presenting the campus projects for accreditation and overseeing their implementation once approved. A national commission, comprising representatives from regional authorities, the Ministry of Education and Youth, and other governmental bodies, grants labels to campuses for a period of one to five years. This label certifies that a campus meets rigorous standards for excellence in education and training. Additionally, the campuses are closely integrated with local businesses and regional development policies, allowing them to serve as hubs of innovation and skills development. This governance model ensures that the campuses remain adaptable to regional economic priorities and the evolving demands of the workforce.

Lifelong Learning Catalyst in the Netherlands

In the Netherlands, the government commissioned a consortium of five research institutes (KBA-Consortium) to prepare an independent review of the VET, higher education and research sectors to identify a vision for 2040. In its final report, the Consortium identifies climate change as one of several key societal challenges around which the government should foster collaboration between the three sectors (KBA-Consortium, 2023[92]). Five recommendations are made to support such collaboration: 1) promoting equal opportunities for all students; 2) strengthening the connection between education and the labour market; 3) strengthening the role of the regions; 4) creating parity of esteem between VET providers, universities of applied science (UAS) and universities; and 5) science engagement and communication.

To progress the implementation of these recommendations, one concrete action of the government has been to provide financial support for the establishment of the Lifelong Learning Catalyst (*LLO Katalysator*), a national platform to co-ordinate and fund the development of—among others—regionally anchored dual sector provision tailored to the transition to net zero. In April 2022, following recommendations from the Advisory Committee of the National Growth Fund (*Adviescommissie Nationaal Groeifonds*), the government of the Netherlands mobilised €391.6 million for the establishment of a Lifelong Learning Catalyst (*LLL Catalyser*). The National Growth Fund is one of the Netherlands' main policy instruments through which the government funds projects that can support structural and sustainable economic growth across a range of sectors, including education.

The LLL Catalyst was initiated by the sectoral associations for VET providers (*MBO Raad*), universities of applied sciences (*Vereniging Hogescholen*) and universities (*Universiteiten van Nederland*), as well as a wide consortium of employers and public sector organisations. It seeks to support the creation of regional and sectoral "LLL-ecosystems" in which employers and education providers collaborate to develop accessible and labour market-relevant courses to support upskilling and re-skilling. The network offers sectoral support for this through four main activities: 1) mapping skills for the future; 2) funding projects focused on specific priorities (until 2026, "solutions for the green transition" is the theme under which the platform will collect applications); 3) capacity building and professional development of staff; and 4) stimulating lifelong learning cultures in companies. After two subsidy rounds, 70 projects or public-private partnerships have now started in regions throughout the Netherlands, focusing on the energy and raw materials transition.

Tertiary Pathfinders in Scotland

In Scotland (United Kingdom), in 2022, the government set up Regional Delivery Boards (RDB) for two "Tertiary Pathfinder" regions, in the north and south-east of the country. The RDBs include representatives from VET providers and HEIs, employers and other actors in the regional skills ecosystem. They oversee the implementation of seven pilot projects focused on improving the alignment of post-16 provision with local and regional skills and more integrated pathways from school through to degree-level provision (SFC, 2022[93]). Several pilots also focus on the green transition. For example, the pilot on Energy Careers Pathways focuses on improving communication of low-carbon energy jobs and the education pathways into them. In another pilot, Scotland's Rural and Borders Colleges collaborate to identify and jointly develop land-based provision, including agriculture or countryside and wildlife management.

Source: Adapted from LLL Catalyser (n.d.[94]), LLO Katalysator [LLL Catalyser], https://www.llokatalysator.nl/ and Government of the Netherlands (2023[95]) (accessed on 6 December 2024), Staatscourant van het Koninkrijk der Nederlanden [Government gazette of the Kingdom of the Netherlands], Government of the Netherlands, https://zoek.officielebekendmakingen.nl/stcrt-2023-19046.html. (accessed on 6 December 2024); Regional Tertiary Pathfinders, Scottish Funding Council (SFC), Edinburgh, https://www.sfc.ac.uk/skills-lifelong-learning/pathfinders/ (accessed on 18 July 2024).

Supporting VET and higher education providers in enhancing the lifelong learning offer

Expanding lifelong learning offerings remains a challenge for many VET and higher education systems. For HEIs, one of the main reasons for this is because their primary focus continues to be to attract upper-secondary school enrolment in traditional bachelor's and master's programmes. In addition, lifelong learning is often not explicitly mentioned in legislation as a mission of VET providers and HEIs. According to the OECD Higher Education Policy Survey 2022, only six out of 29 responding jurisdictions legally mandate some or all HEIs to provide upskilling or re-skilling (OECD, 2024[49]). This has an impact on associated funding systems and limits institutions' ambitions to making lifelong learning an integral part of their activities. Giving institutions a clear mandate for the integration of flexible upskilling and re-skilling opportunities in their study programmes is thus crucial. In VET, some countries have adapted their systems to make them more flexible for adult learners; others (such as Denmark) have created separate tracks for adult learners (OECD, 2023[45]).

To incentivise the development of lifelong learning opportunities, governments may also provide funding to education providers to cover some of the initial costs associated with the development of new delivery formats. Such funding is often targeted to certain policy priorities, such as enhancing labour-market relevance and social inclusion more broadly, or to support upskilling and re-skilling in greening sectors specifically. In Europe, several countries are using EU Recovery and Resilience Facility (RRF) funding to support the development of upskilling and re-skilling courses for the green transition (European Commission, 2022[96]). In Slovenia, for example, the Ministry of Higher Education, Science and Innovation (MVZI) has invested EUR 55.6 million of RRF funding in 38 pilot projects, implemented by four public HEIs, to support a "Reform Higher Education for a Green and Resilient Transition to Society 5.0" (Republic of Slovenia, 2024[97]). To support HEIs with the development of their pilot projects, the Ministry developed a set of guidelines, covering three broad thematic areas: 1) the digital transition, 2) the green transition and 3) lifelong learning, including micro-credentials.

In some countries, the transition to a more flexible lifelong learning offering in VET and higher education is further supported by (voluntary) external review services offered by the external quality assurance (QA) agency or inspectorate. Through such services, VET and higher education providers can obtain advice on the quality and relevance of their course offerings and improve their effectiveness (Staring and Butler, forthcoming[62]). In Estonia, for example, the Quality Agency for Education (HAKA) offers a voluntary external review service for digital courses. The service was developed in the wake of the COVID-19 pandemic, is open to teaching staff and providers from all levels of education, and works as an incentive for VET providers and HEIs to develop more flexible and accessible courses (HAKA, 2021[98]). Similarly, the Dutch-Flemish Accreditation Organisation (NVAO) in the Netherlands offers a special assessment of small-scale and intensive education, as well as sustainable higher education (see Box 3.8).

Box 3.8. Voluntary "special feature" assessment of small-scale and intensive provision and sustainable higher education in the Netherlands

NVAO is responsible for the external evaluation and accreditation of all higher education providers and programmes in the Netherlands and the Flemish Community of Belgium. For Dutch HEIs, NVAO offers "special feature" assessment of programmes in four areas of strategic importance for the government and higher education sector: internationalisation, entrepreneurship, sustainable higher education, and small-scale and intensive provision. The sustainability area is for programmes that wish to integrate content related to the Sustainable Development Goals with their existing programmes and make it relevant to the sectors that they are preparing learners for.

The evaluation procedure involves a self-evaluation by the institution of the selected strategic area ("special feature") in relation to its programme (e.g. how sustainability is integrated and addressed in the existing course offer), followed by a review and site visit by an external expert panel. Based on the self-assessment report and site visit, the external review panel prepares a report with recommendations for the institution on how they can improve the quality and effectiveness of their provision in relation to the special feature under examination. The special assessment is free of charge when it is part of the regular, six-yearly external assessments of study programmes, which is mandatory for all publicly funded HEIs in the Netherlands. For a separate assessment, the fee is EUR 1 000.

Source: NVAO (2024[99]), Special Features General, Dutch-Flemish Accreditation Organisation (NVAO), https://www.nvao.net/en/procedures/the-netherlands/special-features-general (accessed on 06 December 2024)

Supporting VET and higher education teachers in keeping up with the green transition

In addition to developing opportunities for the broader adult workforce to engage in lifelong learning, specific attention needs to be paid to the upskilling and re-skilling of those who are teaching in VET and higher education institutions. Given the rapid changes brought to labour markets, sectors and skills requirements by the green transition, supporting educators in VET and higher education to invest in continuing professional learning (CPL) can also play an important role in keeping their own knowledge and skills up to date.

For VET teachers, it is common to be required to hold a teaching qualification, vocational qualification and/or work experience, although requirements differ across countries as well as between different programmes and subjects taught. Typically, in-company trainers will be required to have a relevant vocational qualification and work experience, but dedicated training for in-company trainers is less common, although it does exist in some countries. In Canada, Denmark, Estonia, the Netherlands and Norway, for example, in-company trainers are required to have a vocational qualification and demonstrate a certain number of years of professional experience to ensure quality (OECD, 2022[100]). In Germany and Switzerland, in-company trainers require a specific training qualification. Data from the OECD's Teaching and Learning International Survey (TALIS) also found that VET teachers feel less prepared than those from general programmes to support their students to adapt to global megatrends such as digitalisation or the transition to a low-carbon economy specifically (OECD, 2021[101]). CPL is crucial for VET teachers to ensure that they keep abreast of changes in the labour market, including those resulting from the green transition.

Higher education faces a similar challenge of raising the bar for teaching staff's general pedagogical competencies. Beyond holding a PhD qualification, it is not common for academic staff to hold any type of formal teaching qualification or to engage in CPL. In countries where such requirements do exist, this is often not centrally regulated and the nature of teaching requirements is determined by individual institutions, or limited to professional HEIs, as is the case in the French Community of Belgium or Switzerland (OECD, 2024[102]). In Denmark and the Netherlands, agreements negotiated between HEIs specify minimum competence requirements for all academic staff involved in teaching, but these primarily focus on basic pedagogical skills (VSNU, 2008[103]; Universities Denmark, 2021[104]).

In some higher education systems, dedicated national supports have been created to support CPL of higher education teaching staff, including on sustainability matters. For example, Ireland's National Forum for the Enhancement of Teaching and Learning leads and advises on the enhancement of teaching and learning in Irish higher education. In 2022-24, the activities of the forum centre on three key priorities, one of which is education for sustainable development (Ireland's National Forum for the Enhancement of Teaching and Learning in Higher Education, 2022[105]).

In the European context, a major initiative bringing together the VET and higher education sectors around CPL is the Centres of Vocational Excellence (CoVE) scheme. CoVEs seek to promote vocational excellence in Europe, which is defined as "high-quality training and education, but also to [enhance] relevance to the world of work and the attractiveness of the educational offer to learners and to employers" (EC, 2024[106]). This is done by fostering the development of local skills ecosystems in which VET providers, HEIs and employers collaborate around common skills challenges. A mapping of CoVEs has found that such centres typically seek to support VET providers and teachers with the development and implementation of innovative teaching and learning methods, project-based learning, the integration of transversal and technical skills in curricula, and sharing facilities between VET and higher education institutions (EC, 2019[107]).

Box 3.9. Centres of Vocational Excellence to support skills development for a greener Europe

GREENOVET is an international project, co-funded by the EU's Erasmus+ programme, supporting the development of the knowledge, resources and infrastructure needed to support innovation and skills ecosystems, regional development, and promoting environmental, social, and economic progress in four regions: Styria (Austria), Vaasa (Finland), Skopje (Macedonia) and Leiria (Portugal).

The CoVEs foster collaboration among a wide range of stakeholders in each region: regional upper-secondary and higher VET providers, local companies, sector and employer representatives, regional and national governments, as well as regional innovation agencies. Through the organisation of conferences, workshops and strategic research, the CoVEs seek to align stakeholders around common challenges and enablers for green skills development in each region, as well as Europe more broadly.

Source: Adapted from (GREENOVET, n.d.[108]), *GREENOVET: Skills for a Green Europe*, https://www.greenovet.eu/ (accessed on 8 August 2024)

References

AK (2024), *Bildungskarenz*, Arbeiterkammer (AK) Österreich [Austrian Chamber of Workers and Employees], Vienna, https://www.arbeiterkammer.at/beratung/bildung/bildungsfoerderungen/Bildungskarenz.html#:~:text=Die%20Mindestdauer%20der%20Bildungskarenz%20betr%C3%A4gt,mindestens%20zwei%20Monate%20umfassen%20muss. (accessed on 22 April 2024). [111]

Anthony Irving, B. and B. Malik Liévano (2019), "Ecojustice, equity and ethics: challenges for educational and career guidance.", *Revista Fuentes*, Vol. 21/2, pp. 253-263, https://doi.org/10.12795/revistafuentes.2019.v21.i2.09. [41]

Australian Department of Education (2024), *Australian Universities Accord - Final Report*, Australian Department of Education, https://www.education.gov.au/australian-universities-accord/resources/final-report (accessed on 17 July 2024). [66]

Auzinger, M., D. Ulicna and K. Messerer (2016), *Study on higher Vocational Education and Training in the EU*, European Commission, Brussels, https://doi.org/10.2767/421741 (accessed on 16 May 2024). [84]

BMBWF (2022), *Nationaler Implementierungsplan (NIP) Österreich [National Implementation Plan (NIP) Austria]*, Ministry of Education, Science and Training (BMBWF), Ministry of Digitalisation and Labour Market (BMDW), https://ec.europa.eu/social/BlobServlet?docId=26326&langId=en (accessed on 31 July 2024). [74]

Borgonovi, F. et al. (2023), "The effects of the EU Fit for 55 package on labour markets and the demand for skills", *OECD Social, Employment and Migration Working Papers*, No. 297, OECD Publishing, Paris, https://doi.org/10.1787/6c16baac-en. [16]

Carosin, E. and D. Canzittu (2019), "A reflection on career guidance skills for the 21st century in a Guidance Oriented Approach to Learning (GOAL)", Vol. 8, pp. 375-391, https://doi.org/10.34862/sp.2019.8. [42]

Causa, O., M. Nguyen and E. Soldani (2024), "Lost in the green transition? Measurement and stylized facts", *OECD Economics Department Working Papers*, No. 1796, OECD Publishing, Paris, https://doi.org/10.1787/dce1d5fe-en. [6]

Causa, O. et al. (2024), "Labour markets transitions in the greening economy: Structural drivers and the role of policies", *OECD Economics Department Working Papers*, No. 1803, OECD Publishing, Paris, https://doi.org/10.1787/d8007e8f-en. [15]

Cedefop (2021), *The green employment and skills transformation: insights from a European Green Deal skills forecast scenario*, http://data.europa.eu/doi/10.2801/112540 (accessed on 12 September 2024). [115]

Cedefop (2012), *Green skills and environmental awareness in vocational education and training*, Publication Office, Luxemburg, https://www.cedefop.europa.eu/files/5524_en.pdf (accessed on 2 July 2024). [24]

Cedefop (n.d.), *Skills forecast countries reports*, https://www.cedefop.europa.eu/en/country-reports/skills-forecasts?page=0 (accessed on 12 September 2024). [33]

Chang, Y. and A. Mann (2024), "Enhancing green career guidance systems for sustainable futures", *OECD Education Working Papers*, No. 318, OECD Publishing, Paris, https://doi.org/10.1787/e6ad2d9c-en. [39]

Clare, J. (2023), *New microcredential courses to support in-demand jobs*, Ministers' Media Centre, https://ministers.education.gov.au/clare/new-microcredential-courses-support-demand-jobs (accessed on 29 June 2023). [88]

Climate University (2023), *Climate University: Teaching and Learning for Sustainable Future*, https://blogs.helsinki.fi/climateuniversity/ (accessed on 10 June 2023). [81]

Council of the EU (2009), *The European Qualifications Framework for lifelong learning*, Council of Ministers of the European Union (EU), Brussels, https://eur-lex.europa.eu/legal-content/EN/TXT/PDF/?uri=CELEX:32017H0615(01) (accessed on 31 July 2024). [69]

Dechezleprêtre, A. et al. (2022), "Fighting climate change: International attitudes toward climate policies", *OECD Economics Department Working Papers*, No. 1714, OECD Publishing, Paris, https://doi.org/10.1787/3406f29a-en. [13]

DESE (2023), *Professional Learning Through Micro-Credentials*, Division of Elementary and Secondary Education (DESE), https://dese.ade.arkansas.gov/Offices/educator-effectiveness/educator-support--development/professional-learning-through-micro-credentials#:~:text=What%20are%20micro%2Dcredentials%3F,trained%20assessors%20against%20a%20rubric. (accessed on 28 June 2023). [114]

Dowling, A. (2015), *The Dowling Review of Business-University Research Collaborations*, https://www.gov.uk/government/publications/business-university-research-collaborations-dowling-review-final-report. [59]

EC (2024), *Centres of Vocational Excellence*, European Commission, Brussels, https://ec.europa.eu/social/main.jsp?catId=1501 (accessed on 28 April 2024). [106]

EC (2024), *Industrial Ecosystems and Partnerships*, European Commission, Brussels, https://pact-for-skills.ec.europa.eu/about/industrial-ecosystems-and-partnerships_en (accessed on 30 July 2024). [91]

EC (2020), *Osnabrück Declaration on vocational education and training as an enabler of recovery and just transitions to digital and green economies*, European Commission, Brussels, https://ec.europa.eu/social/main.jsp?catId=738&langId=en&pubId=8441&furtherPubs=yes (accessed on 31 July 2024). [73]

EC (2019), *Mapping of Centres of Vocational Excellence (CoVEs)*, Publications Office of the European Union, Luxembourg, https://op.europa.eu/en/publication-detail/-/publication/566920f4-ee2d-11e9-a32c-01aa75ed71a1/language-en (accessed on 28 April 2024). [107]

Eckel, P. (2023), "The Trouble With Strategy", https://www.insidehighered.com/opinion/career-advice/2023/05/23/trouble-strategy (accessed on 22 December 2023). [72]

Ehlers, U. and L. Eigbrecht (2024), *Creating the University of the Future: A Global View on Future Skills and Future Higher Education*, Zukunft der Hochschulbildung [Future Higher Education], Karlsruhe, https://link.springer.com/book/10.1007/978-3-658-42948-5 (accessed on 30 July 2024). [53]

ESCO (2022), "Green Skills and Knowledge Concepts: Labelling the ESCO classification", https://esco.ec.europa.eu/system/files/2023-07/Green%20Skills%20and%20Knowledge%20-%20Labelling%20ESCO.pdf. [25]

European Commission (2023), *Green deal industrial plan - plugging the skills gap*, https://year-of-skills.europa.eu/document/download/66dd95df-21b1-44f4-98c3-95af6addbdd8_en?filename=Skills4Green_factsheet_EN_07022024.pdf (accessed on 4 July 2024). [9]

European Commission (2022), *Recovery and Resilience Facility*, European Commission, https://ec.europa.eu/info/business-economy-euro/recovery-coronavirus/recovery-and-resilience-facility_en#the-recovery-and-resilience-facility (accessed on 27 November 2022). [96]

European Commission (2018), *The state of university-business cooperation in Europe*, https://doi.org/10.2766/676478. [60]

European Investment Bank (EIB) (2023), *Investment Report 2022/2023: Resilience and renewal in Europe*. [10]

French Ministry of Education and Youth (2024), *La Validation des Acquis de l'Expérience (VAE) [Recognition of Prior Learning {RPL)]*, https://www.education.gouv.fr/la-validation-des-acquis-de-l-experience-vae-3077#:~:text=Fonctionnement%20de%20la%20VAE,-La%20VAE%20permet&text=Le%20candidat%20doit%20remplir%20un,ou%20partie%20du%20dipl%C3%B4me%20vis%C3%A9. (accessed on 6 August 2024). [86]

Gonzales Ehlinger, E. and F. Stephany (2023), "Skills or Degree? The Rise of Skill-Based Hiring for AI and Green Jobs", https://papers.ssrn.com/sol3/papers.cfm?abstract_id=4665577. [52]

Government of Australia (2022), *National Microcredentials Framework*, Australian Department of Education, https://www.education.gov.au/higher-education-publications/resources/national-microcredentials-framework (accessed on 12 October 2022). [87]

Government of Singapore (2024), *SkillsFuture Credit*, https://www.skillsfuture.gov.sg/initiatives/mid-career/credit#:~:text=Opening%20SkillsFuture%20Credit%20of%20%24500,opening%20credit%20of%20S%24500 (accessed on 22 April 2024). [77]

Government of the Netherlands (2023), *Staatscourant van het Koninkrijk der Nederlanden [Government gazette of the Kingdomof the Netherlands]*, Government of the Netherlands, https://zoek.officielebekendmakingen.nl/stcrt-2023-19046.html (accessed on 19 July 2024). [95]

Grashof, N. and S. Basilico (2024), "Divergent paths for green transition: regional disparities in technology diversification", *Regional Studies*, pp. 1-17, https://doi.org/10.1080/00343404.2024.2363327. [18]

GREENOVET (n.d.), *GREENOVET: Skills for a Green Europe*, https://www.greenovet.eu/ (accessed on 8 August 2024). [108]

HAKA (2021), *Guidelines for the e-course quality label*, Estonian Quality Agency for Education (HAKA), Tallinn, https://haka.ee/wp-content/uploads/Guidelines-E-course-QL2021_EN.pdf (accessed on 5 August 2024). [98]

HEA (2023), *System Performance Framework 2023-2028*, Higher Education Authority (HEA), Dublin, https://hea.ie/assets/uploads/2017/04/System_Performance_Framework_2023-2028.pdf (accessed on 23 July 2024). [68]

Hungarian Parliament (2023), *2013. évi LXXVII. törvény a felnőttképzésről [LXXVII of 2013 law about adult education]*, https://njt.hu/jogszabaly/2013-77-00-00.17 (accessed on 5 August 2024). [89]

IEA (2023), *World Energy Employment 2023*, https://www.iea.org/reports/world-energy-employment-2023. [109]

IEA (2022), *Skills Development and Inclusivity for Clean Energy Transitions*, IEA, Paris, https://www.iea.org/reports/skills-development-and-inclusivity-for-clean-energy-transitions, Licence: CC BY 4.0 (accessed on 5 July 2024). [35]

International Labour Organization (2023), *World employment and social outlook*, ILO, Geneva, https://doi.org/10.54394/sncp1637. [8]

IPCC (2023), *Climate Change 2023: Synthesis Report. Contribution of Working Groups I, II and III to the Sixth Assessment Report of the Intergovernmental Panel on Climate Change [Core Writing Team, H. Lee and J. Romero (eds.)]. IPCC, Geneva, Switzerland.*, IPCC, Geneva, Switzerland, https://doi.org/10.59327/IPCC/AR6-9789291691647. [26]

Ireland's National Forum for the Enhancement of Teaching and Learning in Higher Education (2022), *Strategic Alignment of Teaching and Learning Enhancement Funding in Higher Education 2022/23*, https://www.teachingandlearning.ie/funding/#1656579866344-e65fbc82-6c26 (accessed on 15 November 2023). [105]

Jongbloed, B. et al. (2022), *Final report of the study on the state and effectiveness of national funding systems of higher education to support the European universities initiative . Volume I*, Publications Office of the European Union, Luxembourg, https://op.europa.eu/en/publication-detail/-/publication/dfd61c3c-c79c-11ed-a05c-01aa75ed71a1/language-en (accessed on 19 July 2024). [63]

Kato, S., V. Galán-Muros and T. Weko (2020), "The emergence of alternative credentials", *OECD Education Working Papers*, No. 216, OECD Publishing, Paris, https://doi.org/10.1787/b741f39e-en. [46]

KBA-Consortium (2023), *Vandaag is het 2040: Toekomstverkenning voor middelbaar beroepsonderwijs, hoger onderwijs en wetenschap [Today it is 2040: Exploration of the future for VET, higher education and science]*, Dutch Ministry of Education, Culture and Science, https://www.rijksoverheid.nl/documenten/rapporten/2023/09/08/toekomstverkenning-voor-middelbaar-beroepsonderwijs-hoger-onderwijs-en-wetenschap-deel-1 (accessed on 18 July 2024). [92]

Keese, M. and L. Marcolin (2023), "Labour and social policies for the green transition: A conceptual framework", *OECD Social, Employment and Migration Working Papers*, No. 295, OECD Publishing, Paris, https://doi.org/10.1787/028ffbeb-en. [36]

Kis, V. and H. Windisch (2018), "Making skills transparent: Recognising vocational skills acquired through workbased learning", *OECD Education Working Papers*, No. 180, OECD Publishing, Paris, https://doi.org/10.1787/5830c400-en. [78]

Kompetansebehovsutvalget (2023), *Utfordringer for grønn omstilling i arbeidslivet*, https://kompetansebehovsutvalget.no/wp-content/uploads/2023/09/KBU-temarapport-2023.pdf (accessed on 12 September 2024). [32]

Lim, J., M. Aklin and M. Frank (2023), "Location is a major barrier for transferring US fossil fuel employment to green jobs", *Nature Communications*, Vol. 14/1, https://doi.org/10.1038/s41467-023-41133-9. [17]

LinkedIn (2024), *Global Green Skills Report 2023*, https://economicgraph.linkedin.com/content/dam/me/economicgraph/en-us/global-green-skills-report/green-skills-report-2023.pdf (accessed on 6 July 2024). [4]

LLL Catalyser (n.d.), *LLO Katalysator [LLL Catalyser]*, https://www.llokatalysator.nl/ (accessed on 1 August 2024). [94]

McGrath, J. (2023), "What systematic connections should we have around schools to support the work of teachers? : Global lessons and the potential of ambition loops | Documents de travail de l'OCDE sur l'éducation | OECD iLibrary", *OECD Education Working Papers No. 296*, https://www.oecd-ilibrary.org/fr/education/what-systematic-connections-should-we-have-around-schools-to-support-the-work-of-teachers_77de597c-en (accessed on 10 June 2023). [113]

Millward, C. (2023), *What does the tertiary turn in higher education policy mean in practice?*, https://wonkhe.com/blogs/what-does-the-tertiary-turn-in-higher-education-policy-mean-in-practice/ (accessed on 12 July 2024). [21]

NVAO (2024), *Special Features General*, Dutch-Flemish Accreditation Organisation (NVAO), https://www.nvao.net/en/procedures/the-netherlands/special-features-general (accessed on 5 August 2024). [99]

OECD (2024), *Challenging Social Inequality Through Career Guidance: Insights from International Data and Practice*, OECD Publishing, Paris, https://doi.org/10.1787/619667e2-en. [44]

OECD (2024), "Cultivating green futures: Helping students understand and progress towards green jobs", *OECD Education Policy Perspectives*, No. 104, OECD Publishing, Paris, https://doi.org/10.1787/7c9912c5-en. [43]

OECD (2024), "Cultivating the next generation of green and digital innovators: The role of higher education", *OECD Education Policy Perspectives*, No. 95, OECD Publishing, Paris, https://doi.org/10.1787/bb6e432e-en. [47]

OECD (2024), *Development Co-operation Report 2024: Tackling Poverty and Inequalities through the Green Transition*, OECD Publishing, Paris, https://doi.org/10.1787/357b63f7-en. [12]

OECD (2024), *OECD Employment Outlook 2024: The Net-Zero Transition and the Labour Market*, OECD Publishing, Paris, https://doi.org/10.1787/ac8b3538-en. [3]

OECD (2024), "Promoting green and digital innovation: The role of upskilling and reskilling in higher education", *OECD Education Policy Perspectives*, No. 103, OECD Publishing, Paris, https://doi.org/10.1787/feb029df-en. [49]

OECD (2024), "The state of academic careers in OECD countries: An evidence review", *OECD Education Policy Perspectives No. 91*, https://doi.org/10.1787/5cc2d673-en (accessed on 1 March 2024). [102]

OECD (2023), *Assessing and Anticipating Skills for the Green Transition: Unlocking Talent for a Sustainable Future*, Getting Skills Right, OECD Publishing, Paris, https://doi.org/10.1787/28fa0bb5-en. [31]

OECD (2023), *Building Future-Ready Vocational Education and Training Systems*, OECD Reviews of Vocational Education and Training, OECD Publishing, Paris, https://doi.org/10.1787/28551a79-en. [45]

OECD (2023), "Education and innovation for the digital and green transitions: How higher education can support effective curricula in schools", *OECD Education Policy Perspectives*, https://doi.org/10.1787/5cc2d673-en. [57]

OECD (2023), *Education Policy Outlook 2023: Empowering All Learners to Go Green*, OECD Publishing, Paris, https://doi.org/10.1787/f5063653-en. [7]

OECD (2023), *Ensuring Quality Digital Higher Education in Hungary*, OECD Publishing, Paris, https://doi.org/10.1787/5f44fd6f-en (accessed on 5 April 2023). [90]

OECD (2023), *Flexible adult learning provision: What it is, why it matters,*, OECD Publishing, Paris, https://www.oecd.org/els/emp/skills-and-work/adult-learning/booklet-flexibility-2023.pdf (accessed on 16 May 2024). [85]

OECD (2023), *Flexible adult learning provision: What it is, why it matters, and how to make it work*, OECD Publishing, Paris, https://www.oecd.org/content/dam/oecd/en/topic/policy-sub-issues/adult-learning/booklet-flexibility-2023.pdf (accessed on 1 August 2024). [82]

OECD (2023), *Job Creation and Local Economic Development 2023: Bridging the Great Green Divide*, OECD Publishing, Paris, https://doi.org/10.1787/21db61c1-en. [5]

OECD (2023), *OECD Regional Outlook 2023: The Longstanding Geography of Inequalities*, OECD Publishing, Paris, https://doi.org/10.1787/92cd40a0-en. [19]

OECD (2023), *OECD Skills Outlook 2023: Skills for a Resilient Green and Digital Transition*, OECD Publishing, Paris, https://doi.org/10.1787/27452f29-en. [14]

OECD (2023), *PISA 2022 Results (Volume I): The State of Learning and Equity in Education*, PISA, OECD Publishing, Paris, https://doi.org/10.1787/53f23881-en. [37]

OECD (2023), *Policy Questionnaire: Adult Learning for the Green Transition*. [40]

OECD (2023), *Public policies for effective micro-credential learning*, OECD Publishing, Paris. [48]

OECD (2023), *Strengthening Upper Secondary Education in Lithuania*, OECD Publishing, Paris, https://doi.org/10.1787/a69409d7-en. [110]

OECD (2022), *Declaration on Building Equitable Societies Through Education*, https://legalinstruments.oecd.org/en/instruments/OECD-LEGAL-0485 (accessed on 14 June 2024). [1]

OECD (2022), *Declaration on Building Equitable Societies Through Education*, OECD Publishing, Paris, https://legalinstruments.oecd.org/en/instruments/OECD-LEGAL-0485 (accessed on 19 January 2023). [56]

OECD (2022), *Equitable Framework and Finance for Extractive-based Countries in Transition (EFFECT)*, OECD Development Policy Tools, OECD Publishing, Paris, https://doi.org/10.1787/7871c0ad-en. [22]

OECD (2022), *Pathways to Professions: Understanding Higher Vocational and Professional Tertiary Education Systems*, OECD Reviews of Vocational Education and Training, OECD Publishing, Paris, https://doi.org/10.1787/a81152f4-en. [54]

OECD (2022), *Policies to Support Green Entrepreneurship: Building a Hub for Green Entrepreneurship in Denmark*, OECD Studies on SMEs and Entrepreneurship, OECD Publishing, Paris, https://doi.org/10.1787/e92b1946-en. [55]

OECD (2022), *Preparing Vocational Teachers and Trainers: Case Studies on Entry Requirements and Initial Training*, OECD Publishing, Paris, https://doi.org/10.1787/c44f2715-en (accessed on 8 August 2024). [100]

OECD (2022), *What Students Learn Matters: Towards a 21st Century Curriculum*, OECD Publishing, Paris, https://www.oecd-ilibrary.org/education/what-students-learn-matters_d86d4d9a-en (accessed on 1 March 2023). [70]

OECD (2021), *Career Guidance for Adults in a Changing World of Work*, Getting Skills Right, OECD Publishing, Paris, https://doi.org/10.1787/9a94bfad-en. [38]

OECD (2021), *OECD Skills Outlook 2021: Learning for Life*, OECD Publishing, Paris, https://doi.org/10.1787/0ae365b4-en. [27]

OECD (2021), *Teachers and Leaders in Vocational Education and Training*, OECD Publishing, Paris, https://doi.org/10.1787/59d4fbb1-en (accessed on 8 August 2024). [101]

OECD (2020), *Curriculum Overload: A Way Forward*, OECD Publishing, Paris, https://doi.org/10.1787/3081ceca-en. [71]

OECD (2020), *TALIS 2018 Results (Volume I): Teachers and School Leaders as Lifelong Learners*, OECD Publishing, Paris, https://www.oecd.org/education/talis-2018-results-volume-i-1d0bc92a-en.htm (accessed on 17 March 2023). [112]

OECD (2019), *Benchmarking Higher Education System Performance*, Higher Education, OECD Publishing, Paris, https://doi.org/10.1787/be5514d7-en (accessed on 28 July 2023). [51]

OECD (2019), *Getting Skills Right: Creating responsive adult learning systems*, https://www.oecd.org/content/dam/oecd/en/topics/policy-sub-issues/adult-learning/adult-learning-systems-2019.pdf (accessed on 2 July 2024). [34]

OECD (2019), "Getting Skills Right: Engaging low-skilled adults in learning", https://www.oecd.org/employment/emp/engaging-low-skilled-adults-2019.pdf (accessed on 22 April 2024). [80]

OECD (2019), *Getting Skills Right: Future-Ready Adult Learning Systems*, Getting Skills Right, OECD Publishing, Paris, https://doi.org/10.1787/9789264311756-en. [79]

OECD (2017), *Getting Skills Right: Skills for Jobs Indicators*, Getting Skills Right, OECD Publishing, Paris, https://doi.org/10.1787/9789264277878-en. [30]

OECD (2016), *Getting Skills Right: Assessing and Anticipating Changing Skill Needs*, Getting Skills Right, OECD Publishing, Paris, https://doi.org/10.1787/9789264252073-en. [29]

OECD (2008), *Tertiary Education for the Knowledge Society*, OECD Publishing, Paris, https://www.oecd.org/education/skills-beyond-school/41266690.pdf (accessed on 6 June 2023). [50]

OECD (2024, forthcoming), *Training provision for the green transition and adoption of AI.* [28]

Republic of Slovenia (2024), *Systemic support for the greening of higher education*, https://www.gov.si/en/registries/projects/e-vodnik-za-ozelenitev-visokega-solstva/dodaj-stran-231201161825/ (accessed on 5 August 2024). [97]

Sabarwal, S. et al. (2024), *Choosing Our Future: Education for Climate Action*, http://documents.worldbank.org/curated/en/099082624160037461/P180005183528c03c1802a1896a79b744ea. [23]

Sam Huckstep and Helen Dempster (2024), *Meeting Skill Needs for the Global Green Transition: A Role for Labour Migration?*, CGD Policy Paper 318, https://www.cgdev.org/publication/meeting-skill-needs-global-green-transition-role-labour-migration (accessed on 25 June 2024). [11]

SFC (2022), *Regional Tertiary Pathfinders*, Scottish Funding Council (SFC), Edinburgh, https://www.sfc.ac.uk/skills-lifelong-learning/pathfinders/ (accessed on 18 July 2024). [93]

SFC (2022), *Strategic Plan 2022-27: Building a connected, agile, sustainable tertiary education and research system for Scotland*, Scottish Funding Council (SFC), Edinburgh, https://www.sfc.ac.uk/wp-content/uploads/uploadedFiles/SFC_StrategicPlan.pdf (accessed on 19 July 2024). [65]

SFC (2021), *Coherence and Sustainability: A Review of Tertiary Education and Research*, Scottish Funding Council (SFC), Edinburgh, https://www.sfc.ac.uk/reform/review/ (accessed on 19 July 2024). [64]

SFS (2024), *Skills Frameworks to support the Industry Transformation Maps*, SkillFuture Singapore (SFS), https://www.skillsfuture.gov.sg/skills-framework (accessed on 18 July 2024). [76]

Singapore Ministry of Education (2023), *Education Statistics Digest 2023*, Singapore Ministry of Education, https://www.moe.gov.sg/-/media/files/about-us/education-statistics-digest-2023.pdf (accessed on 18 July 2024). [75]

SOLAS (2022), *Transforming Learning Strategic Performance Agreements: The Further Education & Training System 2022-2024*, Further Education and Skills Service (SOLAS), Dublin, https://www.solas.ie/f/70398/x/807fb6e096/fet-system-report.pdf (accessed on 24 July 2024). [67]

Staring, F. and S. Butler (forthcoming), *Policies for Effective Quality Assurance in VET and Higher Education*, OECD Education Working Paper No. XX. [58]

Staring, F. and S. Butler (forthcoming), *Policies for Effective Quality Assurance in VET and Higher Education*, OECD Education Working Papers No. XX. [62]

Teo, I. et al. (2023), *International Comparison of Tertiary Education Systems*, Australian Government Department of Education, https://research.acer.edu.au/higher_education/80/ (accessed on 24 June 2024). [20]

Tuck, R. (2007), *An Introductory Guide to National Qualifications Frameworks: Conceptual and Practical Issues for Policy Makers*, International Labour Organisation, Geneva, https://webapps.ilo.org/wcmsp5/groups/public/@ed_emp/@ifp_skills/documents/instructionalmaterial/wcms_103623.pdf (accessed on 16 May 2024). [83]

Universities Denmark (2021), *Danish framework for advancing university pedagogy*, Universities Denmark, https://dkuni.dk/wp-content/uploads/2021/03/danish-framework-for-advancing-university-pedagogy-1.pdf (accessed on 8 June 2023). [104]

van der Ree, K. (2019), "Encourager les emplois verts : le travail décent dans la transition vers des économies vertes et à faible émission de carbone, Promoting Green Jobs: Decent Work in the Transition to Low-Carbon, Green Economies, Fomento de los empleos verdes: trabajo decente en la transición hacia economías verdes y bajas en carbono", *Revue internationale de politique de développement* 11, pp. 248-271, https://doi.org/10.4000/poldev.3107. [2]

VSNU (2008), *Overeenkomst inzake wederzijdse erkenning basiskwalificatie onderwijs*, VSNU, January 2008, https://www.universiteitenvannederland.nl/files/documenten/BKO-overeenkomst%202018%20BKO%20overeenkomst.pdf (accessed on 1 August 2022). [103]

Withers, J. (2023), *Fit for the Future: developing a post-school learning system to fuel economic transformation. Skills Delivery Landscape Review - Final Report*, Submitted to Scottish Ministers, May 2023. Scottish Government, https://www.gov.scot/binaries/content/documents/govscot/publications/independent-report/2023/06/fit-future-developing-post-school-learning-system-fuel-economic-transformation/documents/fit-future-developing-post-school-learning-system-fuel-economic-transformation-skills-delivery-landscape-review-final-report/fit-future-developing-post-school-learning-system-fuel-economic-transformation-skills-delivery-landscape-review-final-report/govscot%3Adocument/fit-future-developing-post-school-learning-system-fuel-economic-transformation-skills-delivery-landscape-review-final-report.pdf (accessed on 11 July 2024). [61]

Notes

1 Green skills in this definition refer to "the knowledge, abilities, values and attitudes needed to live in, develop and support a society which reduces the impact of human activity on the environment"
2 The full list comprises includes 381 skills, 185 knowledge concepts, and 5 transversal skills as green
3 This section does not include a separate subsection dedicated to sustainability competencies, as these are covered in Chapter 1 and are integrated throughout this chapter, where relevant.
4 Micro-credentials are short, focused courses—often offered online—that are designed to certify knowledge or skills in a specific area, allowing workers to bolster their existing skills set or switch to a new field without needing to commit to a full degree programme.

Annex A. Deep dive: The transition of the energy sector and its implications for skills development

The energy sector plays a pivotal role in the green transition, but the energy transition is off-track a trajectory in line with limiting warming to 1.5°C by 2100, and rapid acceleration of action is needed. The International Energy Agency (IEA)'s 2023 net-zero emissions scenario shows that achieving net-zero CO_2 by 2050 is technically and economically feasible, with key roles being played by renewable energy, energy efficiency and electrification of heat and transport (IEA, 2023[1]). For example, each year, approximately 1,000 GW of renewable power must be installed to be on track for a 1.5°C pathway. In 2022, around 300 GW of renewable capacity was added worldwide, comprising 83% of new installations, while fossil fuels and nuclear power together accounted for only 17% (IRENA, 2023[2]). While the surge of renewables is a positive development, there is a pressing need to significantly further increase renewable capacity and the share of renewables in the electricity mix.

In terms of mitigation, the latest science indicates that net-zero CO_2 energy systems require substantial reductions in fossil fuel use, minimal use of unabated fossil fuels and the adoption of carbon capture, utilisation and storage (CCUS) technologies. This transformation also requires extensive electrification across various sectors, including those less amenable to direct electrification, such as heavy industry, aviation and shipping, alongside the development of alternative energy carriers. Enhancing energy conservation and efficiency measures is crucial, as is integrating various components of the energy system more effectively. This integration will involve, for example, connecting renewable energy sources with energy storage solutions to ensure stability and reliability, especially for intermittent resources like solar and wind. Feasible adaptation options support resilient infrastructure, reliable power systems, and efficient water use across existing and new energy generation systems. Enhanced energy reliability and resilience to climate impacts can be achieved by diversifying energy generation through wind, solar, and small-scale hydropower, coupled with demand-side management initiatives like energy storage and efficiency upgrades. Implementing climate-responsive energy markets and deploying smart-grid technologies, strengthening transmission systems, and bolstering supply response capabilities are all feasible in the medium to long term, offering additional benefits through climate mitigation efforts (IPCC, 2023[3]).

To effectively support the transition towards net-zero CO_2 energy systems, the workforce will require a range of technical skills to meet the demands of this evolving energy landscape. Table A.1 summarises the implications of these potential measures for technical skills demand in this sector.

Table A.1. Examples of mitigation and adaptation measures in the energy sector and implications for technical skills demand

Examples of mitigation and adaptation options	Technical skills needed for achieving these options
• **Fossil Fuel Reduction and Carbon Capture:** Substantial reductions in fossil fuel use; Minimal use of unabated fossil fuels; Adoption of carbon capture and storage technologies. • **Electrification and Alternative Energy:** Extensive electrification across various sectors, including those less amenable to direct electrification; Development of alternative energy carriers. • **Energy Conservation and System Integration:** Enhancing energy conservation and efficiency measures; Effective integration of various components of the energy system. • **Adaptation and Resilience:** Enhancing energy reliability and resilience to climate impacts through diversifying energy generation (wind, solar, small-scale hydropower) and demand-side management initiatives (energy storage, efficiency upgrades). • **Technological and Market Innovations:** Implementing climate-responsive energy markets; Deploying smart-grid technologies; Strengthening transmission systems; Bolstering supply response capabilities; Offering additional benefits through climate mitigation efforts.	• Renewable energy system expertise (wind, solar). • Expertise in installation, maintenance, and operation of renewable energy systems. • Grid integration techniques. • Skills related to carbon capture and storage technology implementation. • Techniques on electrification system operation and maintenance. • Alternative energy carrier development (hydrogen, synthetic fuels, biofuels). • Energy conservation and efficiency optimisation.

Source: Based on IPCC (2023), Climate Change 2023: Synthesis Report. Contribution of Working Groups I, II and III to the Sixth Assessment Report of the Intergovernmental Panel on Climate Change [Core Writing Team, H. Lee and J. Romero (eds.)]. IPCC, Geneva, Switzerland., IPCC, Geneva, Switzerland, https://doi.org/10.59327/IPCC/AR6-9789291691647 (IPCC, 2023[3])

Skilled labour shortages are emerging as a major potential bottleneck for the net-zero transition in the energy sector. Countries emitting 70% of global greenhouse gas emissions have pledged to decarbonise their energy sectors, and in this context, a peak, followed by a decline, in the demand for oil, gas and coal is expected in this current decade. A major shift in energy employment worldwide has been underway since the COVID-19 pandemic, spurred by rapidly growing clean energy investment. Employment in clean energy rose by around 15% between 2019-2023, while fossil fuel-related jobs fell by about 1% over that time. Clean energy already employs more workers than fossil fuels worldwide, and significant growth to 2030 is projected under all scenarios developed by the International Energy Agency (IEA, 2023[4]). Indeed, the energy sector has high job vacancy rates, and with employers struggling to fill positions, skills shortages are already translating into project delays. A lack of workers with energy specialisations is a particular barrier for those companies seeking to fill positions.

This is an issue that requires more attention from policy makers in all regions (see Box A.1 for a discussion of some of these challenges and potential strategic approaches to addressing the skills gap in the energy sector). As most energy jobs are tied to the location where installations are developed – around 60% of energy jobs cannot be offshored – it is essential to develop a sufficiently large and skilled local workforce in every region. Most of the jobs in growing clean energy sectors are in construction and manufacturing, both of which are already facing worker shortages across the broader economy in most parts of the world. Moreover, construction and manufacturing are expected to grow significantly through 2030 in all IEA scenarios, implying a skills bottleneck whose importance is likely to increase. This growth in construction and manufacturing employment varies by region, and the share of construction and manufacturing in total energy employment tends to be higher in developing countries (IEA, 2023[4]).

Taking a global perspective, energy sector transformation is a key pillar of both development processes and the net-zero transition. Developing countries are home to two-thirds of global energy jobs. In particular, the world's largest energy workforce is in Asia, due to factors including its large population, lower labour costs and brisk investment. China has by far the largest national energy labour force, of which clean energy accounts for roughly 60% (IEA, 2023[4]). The global transition to net-zero emissions in the energy sector will thus have a marked impact on labour markets in developing countries.

To date, developing countries have not been able to capture a proportionate share of the benefits of clean energy job growth. Since 2019, over two-thirds of new clean energy jobs have been created in developed countries and China. Employment in clean energy in developing countries (excluding China) grew by 10% from 2019 to 2023, compared to 3% growth in fossil fuel employment. Although the growth in clean energy jobs has been strong, fossil fuel jobs continue to represent a significant share of total energy employment in developing countries (IEA, 2024[5]).

The net-zero transition presents significant challenges for fossil fuel producer developing countries, as they seek to manage their labour markets. The transition risk is particularly acute for coal miners, as coal mines in these countries tend to be less mechanised and rely heavily on unskilled workers. 90% of the coal supply jobs lost in the IEA's net-zero emissions scenario through 2030 are located in developing countries (IEA, 2023[4]). Greening their economies while minimising adverse employment impacts requires well-designed skills policy responses.

Generally lower levels of education and skills availability act as a barrier to more rapid growth in clean energy jobs in developing countries. Companies looking to start or scale up operations in these countries are generally faced with higher costs associated with onboarding and training employees. The fact that many developing countries outside of China have relatively newer and smaller clean energy industries means that even high-skilled workers, where available, are less likely to have the specific experience required by the nascent clean energy industry, and even less likely to be prepared to train others (IEA, 2024[5]).

Careful planning and collaboration between public and private actors is needed to ensure the skills development that will allow developing countries (excluding China) to capture a greater share of clean energy jobs (IEA, 2024[5]). Development finance institutions and other international partners can provide technical and financial assistance to public actors, and to educational and vocational training institutions on the planning, design, and implementation of measures (OECD, 2022[6]). Collaboration with international partners can be useful for skills development through mechanisms such as degree conferrals, training programmes, certification and standard building, curriculum design, and joint ventures and Build-Operate-Transfer agreements. Supporting skills development for the evolving green economy fits well with broader goals of many developing countries of achieving higher youth education levels, formalising the economy, and raising the base skill level of the workforce at large (IEA, 2024[5]).

Box A.1. Addressing the skills gap in the energy sector: challenges and strategic approaches

Analysis conducted by the International Energy Agency (IEA) indicates that the number of workers pursuing degrees or certifications relevant to energy sector jobs is not keeping pace with growing demand. The conferral of relevant science, technology, engineering and mathematics (STEM) degrees is not rising fast enough to meet demand for new workers with these credentials. The gap is even more severe for vocational jobs than for STEM. Vocational education and training (VET) programmes are not expanding fast enough to meet the growing demand in the energy industry. This may in part be due to a poor image of VET among students, along with a lack of understanding of the associated career and salary options. In addition, training courses tailored to energy technologies, particularly newer technologies, are not always available.

To meet the evolving job and skills needs in the energy sector, close co-ordination between governments, agencies, education institutions, industry and workers will be vital. Social dialogue will be important to develop a more responsive and inclusive education system, which would enable low-skilled or underqualified workers to more easily receive additional training and take advantage of these growing opportunities.

There is a need both to integrate new clean energy skills into the curricula of pre-existing certifications and to develop new ones to reflect emerging skill requirements, especially for new industries like carbon capture, utilisation and storage (CCUS) and low-emissions hydrogen. Using skills assessment and anticipation results to update curricula and training programmes is key for these efforts (see also section on Anticipating future skills needs for the green transition). In order to systematically integrate these considerations, National Qualification Frameworks should incorporate skills needed for clean energy as far as possible.

Retraining will be key for enabling the transfer of workers from energy sub-sectors with falling labour needs (e.g. fossil fuels) to growing clean energy sectors. Just under half of the fossil-fuel related job losses from 2023 to 2030 in the IEA NZE Scenario are potentially transferable to new clean energy jobs with retraining (especially workers in oil, gas, and internal combustion engine vehicle manufacturing). However, workers most at risk of displacement are least likely to participate in training. Facilitating access, ensuring affordability, and encouraging participation should be a priority for policymakers. At the same time, workers from fossil fuel sectors cannot address all of the evolving skills demand, and not all workers will be easily transferable with retraining. For instance, workers in coal mining will be challenging to transfer. Previous coal transitions over the past century may offer some policy lessons, including targeted reskilling and community support policies.

Wages in the energy sector are typically higher than pay for similar occupations, reflecting higher skilling and specialisation requirements. Wage premiums in energy continue to attract needed skilled labour. For those requiring additional skills to enter the energy sector, wage premiums must be sufficiently high to incentivise retraining. Government financial support for retraining can help to reduce those premiums needed to attract workers requiring additional skills.

Increasing the number of women entering vocational or educational programmes relevant to energy is an important step to overcoming skills shortages. The share of women awarded STEM bachelor degrees (besides those in biological and medical sciences, where graduates are less likely to work in the energy sector) is gaining some ground, having reached around 29% in the United States, 34% in the European Union, and 44% in India as of 2022. In emerging and developing economies, skilling programmes targeting women can help expand the available labour force and support growing local businesses.

Source: (IEA, 2024[5]) World Energy Employment 2024, https://www.iea.org/reports/world-energy-employment-2024 (accessed on 10 December 2024); (IEA, 2023[1])Net Zero Roadmap: A Global Pathway to Keep the 1.5 °C Goal in Reach, IEA, Paris, https://www.iea.org/reports/net-zero-roadmap-a-global-pathway-to-keep-the-15-0c-goal-in-reach.

References

IEA (2024), *World Energy Employment 2024*, https://www.iea.org/reports/world-energy-employment-2024 (accessed on 10 December 2024). [5]

IEA (2023), *Net Zero Roadmap: A Global Pathway to Keep the 1.5 °C Goal in Reach*, IEA, Paris, https://www.iea.org/reports/net-zero-roadmap-a-global-pathway-to-keep-the-15-0c-goal-in-reach. [1]

IEA (2023), *World Energy Employment 2023*, https://www.iea.org/reports/world-energy-employment-2023. [4]

IPCC (2023), *Climate Change 2023: Synthesis Report. Contribution of Working Groups I, II and III to the Sixth Assessment Report of the Intergovernmental Panel on Climate Change [Core Writing Team, H. Lee and J. Romero (eds.)]. IPCC, Geneva, Switzerland.*, IPCC, Geneva, Switzerland, https://doi.org/10.59327/IPCC/AR6-9789291691647. [3]

IRENA (2023), *World Energy Transitions Outlook 2023: 1.5°C Pathway*, International Renewable Energy Agency, Abu Dhabi. [2]

OECD (2022), *Equitable Framework and Finance for Extractive-based Countries in Transition (EFFECT)*, OECD Development Policy Tools, OECD Publishing, Paris, https://doi.org/10.1787/7871c0ad-en. [6]

www.ingramcontent.com/pod-product-compliance
Lightning Source LLC
Chambersburg PA
CBHW061222240926
51846CB00006B/1318
9789264925168